PRAISE FOR *1% LEADERSHIP*

"Andy has clearly and comprehensively described the lessons of leadership effectively through storytelling guiding continuous improvements on the journey to great leadership. It is not a book to be read once, but is a reference book that should be on everyone's desk."

—JIM NOGA, former CIO, Mass General Brigham

"Why is common sense in such short supply when it's supposed to be, well, common? Andy Ellis takes his years in the trenches of business, across many industries, to fill that void with advice and perspective that any aspiring entrepreneur or executive should use to grow, profit, and inspire their teams not just 1%, but 99.99% of the time."

—PAUL SAGAN, senior advisor, General Catalyst

"Smart, provocative, deceptively simple. In *1% Leadership*, Andy employs his characteristic no-bull approach to coach readers into becoming better leaders, incrementally and authentically."

—AMY BENNETT, editor-in-chief at Foundry
(publishers of CIO, Computerworld, CSO,
InfoWorld, and Network World)

"Every leader learns a million lessons in life, but few are able to succinctly sum them up. In *1% Leadership*, Andy Ellis has done just that. He has masterfully distilled leadership lessons learned over two hard-fought decades into bite-sized chunks that anyone can digest. You'll quickly breeze through his fun, relatable stories, while picking up actionable tips that will improve your life, your team, and your world. Once you read this book, you'll want another copy to give to every aspiring leader you know!"

—SHERRI DAVIDOFF, CEO of LMG Security
and author of *Data Breaches: Crisis and Opportunity*

1%
LEADERSHIP

1%
LEADERSHIP

MASTER THE SMALL,
DAILY IMPROVEMENTS THAT
SET GREAT LEADERS APART

ANDY ELLIS

hachette
BOOKS   *New York*

Hachette Go, an imprint of Hachette Books
Hachette Book Group
1290 Avenue of the Americas
New York, NY 10104
HachetteGo.com
Facebook.com/HachetteGo
Instagram.com/HachetteGo

First Edition: April 2023

Hachette Books is a division of Hachette Book Group, Inc.

The Hachette Go and Hachette Books name and logos are trademarks of
Hachette Book Group, Inc.

The publisher is not responsible for websites (or their content) that are not
owned by the publisher.

Print book interior design by Jeff Williams.

Library of Congress Cataloging-in-Publication Data

Names: Ellis, Andy (Chief information security officer), author.
Title: 1% leadership : master the small, daily improvements that set great leaders apart /
    Andy Ellis. Other titles: One percent leadership
Description: First edition. | New York: Hachette Books, 2023. | Includes index.
Identifiers: LCCN 2022050884 | ISBN 9780306830815 (hardcover) | ISBN
    9780306830839 (ebook)
Subjects: LCSH: Leadership.
Classification: LCC HD57.7 .E4174 2023 | DDC 658.4/092--dc23/eng/20221031
LC record available at https://lccn.loc.gov/2022050884

ISBNs: 9780306830815 (hardcover); 9780306830839 (ebook)

Printed in Canada

MRQ-T

10 9 8 7 6 5 4 3 2 1

To Lila and Isaac,
in recompense for all of the dinner table conversations that
you put up with as I learned to tell these stories, I gift these
tales to you, and someday to your children, as the beginnings
of wisdom that shall always be your inheritance.

May Adonai bless you and keep you.
May Adonai deal kindly and graciously with you.
May Adonai bestow favor upon you and grant you peace.

Contents

Introduction: +1%

HAVE YOU EVER LOOKED CLOSELY AT A CABLE, ROPE, OR BRAID? EACH is made up of strands—seemingly in the thousands—that are, individually, not that impressive. Yet when braided together, they create something inspiringly powerful. Each strand adds just a small bit of strength. That tiny bit of strength is almost meaningless on its own, but, when combined with all of the other tiny strands around it, lends itself to a greater creation.

Leadership is like that. It strikes me that a significant number of business books on management and personal development could be reduced from hundreds of pages to one argument: "If you do X, then amazing things will happen." Each of those arguments is like one strand in a braid of advice, yet pretending to be the entire (and only) rope.

Advice rarely is so powerful as to transform everything about you; instead, it often merely makes a tiny improvement: for some set of people, this advice might improve their expectations of good outcomes, but maybe by no more than 1 percent. How important is that tiny improvement, though? It depends! The difference between the best player in a professional sports league and the worst is just a small collection of tiny effects. But me? A small improvement isn't getting me onto a roster. Understand where there's a cluster effect—maybe a piece of advice is useful, but the biggest effect is seen by people who've already invested in gaining a lot of advantage in a related area, and others might not notice much benefit. If you already have a strong braid, then a few more strands strengthen it even more.

This book aims to provide opportunities for those advantages—giving you 1 percent stronger strands—in a number of related areas of leadership. Each of those opportunities has been provided in a short essay of just a few pages. If an essay doesn't resonate with you, skip it and try another; perhaps you'll come back to it later. If it works for you, practice it until you get that benefit, and then see if you're ready for more. No lesson in here is going to make you a perfect leader; it's going to be the collection of small, incremental improvements that, over time, build your leadership style. Spend a few minutes each Monday morning to focus on one lesson for your leadership development—perhaps that lesson improves your performance by only 1 percent. Practice that lesson for a week. Revisit it from time to time, seeing if you can get 1 percent better at the skill each time you do. It's those accumulated 1 percent improvements that separate the best leaders from everyone else.

I've collected these essays into three sections on leadership. In "Personal Leadership," I've focused on how to think about your own engagement with the world around you; "Team Leadership" is on the nature of interacting with other people, especially those that you lead; and in "Organizational Leadership," I've written about how to strengthen larger, distributed teams. Each essay is as short as possible while still capturing the pertinent message.

Cultural Language

One of the best uses of books in the business world is to assist with the creation of a shared *cultural language*. Organizations will often select a book or training package not just because of its content, but on the strength of the shared language it creates, because language drives culture. When an entire organization starts talking about a specific catchphrase (be it "the growth mind-set," or "hope is not a strategy," or "crossing the chasm"), it serves a number of purposes. It reminds everyone in an organization that this is a known and declared priority for the organization. It puts everyone into a similar frame of mind. It removes the need to spend a lot of time in every interaction rehashing the explanations of those words.

Whatever organizations you're in already have their own cultural language. Some of that language is by design. However, much of it comes about by happenstance, evolving from the independent contributions of many individuals. Learning a new cultural language can be a challenge, for people and organizations. The new language might share vocabulary with existing language, but with different meanings and implications. Confusion arises when people use the same language as shorthands to mean entirely different concepts. Even when the new language doesn't directly conflict with existing language, it still takes practice with the new vocabulary to use it well, fluidly and quickly communicating key concepts without misunderstanding.

If you're reading this alone, recognize that when you take any learnings you might have to others, they might not share the vocabulary of this book with you, and that might limit how much of the 1 percent improvement you can realize. The difference in understanding language can create resistance if you move too quickly. If you're reading this with a group, then practice using the new language together. Create a space where you reinforce your positive journey. Most essays will introduce some phrases for you to consider using to capture the concepts a little more cleanly and help develop that shared cultural language.

A Warning

Here there be dragons.
—ANONYMOUS CARTOGRAPHER

Learning new skills presents challenges. Consider learning to swim. Perhaps you might pick up a book, like this one, and read about the various strokes and core principles about *keeping your head above water* and *not inhaling the water*. It might be filled with pleasant anecdotes about various swimmers and stories about how swimming is a powerful tool that can change your life. Each of those anecdotes will give you a 1 percent improvement to your skills as you learn them.

You learn to swim not by jumping into the deep end, but by learning and practicing each of the individual skills in placid, shallow waters. As you get better, you still continue to practice swimming, because your mastery of skills is never truly complete. Many of the skills in this book are similar. They require practice in small ways, rather than trying to do it all at once.

But.

You don't jump into just any body of water to practice your swimming. The Charles River was toxic until the very end of the twentieth century. Fraser Island is full of rip currents, sharks, and jellyfish. The Orinoco River is rife with piranhas. This isn't just the danger from jumping into the deep end before you can tread water; you might be jumping into a hostile environment that, at best, is indifferent to your continued existence and, at worst, actively wants to eat you. So too with the advice and guidance in this book. In a supportive environment, these ideas can bloom as you practice them. In an unsupportive environment? Some of these ideas can expose you to dangers from hostile colleagues. You'll need to evaluate your environment—it might surprise or shock you—and decide how to proceed.

Talk to your peers, but make sure you listen to your most marginalized teammates about their experiences and how some of these concepts might be received in your environment. Those marginalized teammates might easily recognize many of these essays and be familiar with the environmental dangers they trigger. A number of these skills are, in many organizations, specifically fraught with peril for those marginalized members. The fault lies not in the behaviors, but in the environment, yet it can be hard to quickly tell the difference. For others, practicing these behaviors can expand the safe options for everyone to use them. Consider Chapter 32, "When mistakes happen, don't waste energy blaming people; invest energy in building better systems." For someone who has organizational power, accepting blame to neutralize it is *easy*. For someone at the bottom of the hierarchy, however, accepting blame doesn't necessarily have the same effect and may instead have negative repercussions. In a healthy organization, moving past blame is a powerful approach to organizational improvement, but it takes power to create that safety.

The second section of this book, "Team Leadership," *is* about creating a healthy environment for the people who *will* follow you, so that they can more easily practice all of the lessons in this book and grow a supportive environment. For the first person to break this ground? It's hard work, but it will enable others to extend that environment even further.

If you're a leader, and you want to help your team improve and grow, you *must* accompany them on this journey. If *you* don't demonstrate the behaviors you wish to see from them, visibly, then your team will worry that your insistence on those behaviors is just another form of control. This will feel uncomfortable for you. As a leader, however, *that* discomfort will be less than the discomfort that members of your team feel. You have the power to absorb the costs of failure in ways that others might not. By absorbing those costs, especially when breaking new ground, you lower the costs for those who follow, even if they don't yet see themselves on that path.

Creating that safe path may be thankless for a long time. But it's worth it.

PART I

PERSONAL LEADERSHIP

LEADING YOURSELF—THE ART OF PERSONAL LEADERSHIP—IS ABOUT exploring, and improving, the way that you interact with the world around you. It contains the fundamental building blocks that you'll use in leading others, by forcing you to engage in self-reflection. When you get to the lessons in the later sections of this book, you'll find that many of them are easier to practice if you've already had experience with the related personal skills.

When you hear people talk about authenticity in leadership, that describes the leaders who practice these skills *before* they insist on others using them. You should understand why these skills work for you—and which ones don't—before you blindly suggest them to others.

Great leaders often have a calmness about them, even in moments of chaos or crisis. That calmness creates a place for others to engage with your leadership. It's much easier to radiate that serenity to others if you first practice creating that space for yourself.

1

> Personal improvement is
> a prerequisite to leading
> professionally.

LEADERS. ROLE MODELS. HEROES. THE WORLD IS FILLED WITH human beings that society and culture teach us we should look up to and emulate. But often to our surprise, we learn that each one of them is imperfect because, ultimately, they are all human beings. Our error is in expecting them to be angelic, and perfect, when, like us, they are merely on a path to becoming different versions of themselves.

Hopefully better versions of themselves. Their flaws are often minor, but the more we idolize them, the more extreme those flaws are to us because we feel let down. Our heroes do not always practice what they preach, or they are forced to make trade-offs that we find uncomfortable. At that point, it is easy to turn away from the lessons they offered us. If their wisdom didn't work for them *all the time*, then how could it work for us *at all*? Phrased that extremely, it sounds absurd, but that is often how we judge others.

Because people often look to follow a path to perfection, that absurd question always hangs over us. In seeking the perfect, we sometimes turn away from the lessons that *could* help us, the wisdom that *may* be applicable in some situations, the ideas that we *might* benefit from.

The uncomfortable truth is that there isn't a single formula for leadership. There is no "do this right thing" and people will follow you. The first person you need to lead, though, is yourself. If you aren't able to lead yourself on a journey of improvement, others will have a hard time following your path. When they stumble—and they will stumble, because growth is never seamless—they will need to see that you stumbled, as well. And, more important, that you picked yourself back up and kept improving.

These next essays are all structured around ideas for personal development, but they are ideas that will reflect themselves onto the people around you. Your growth— especially in how you interact with people around you—is the foundation on which your own leadership style can develop. It might be easy to dismiss personal growth as mere self-help, but the people you lead will constrain themselves with your affect. If *you* never seem to have fun, then, implicitly, you've banned fun. If *you* never acknowledge mistakes, then they fear ever being caught making a mistake. This section *is* a self-help guide; it's a set of tools not only to center yourself, but to help you be a more authentic leader.

Some of the tools here will work for you. Some of them have already failed you. But the premise—that leadership begins with *you*—is the first building block, one that will give you a place to stand before you can move the world. The chapters that follow are short essays on personal leadership, on a way of seeing and understanding the world as you walk through it. Most of the essays are just about how you see the world, a few are on how you interact with others, but together they form a guide that helps you become your better self every day and find the bright spots along the way. It isn't about being a shining light to the entire world. It starts by being a light to yourself and then to those around you.

> **Personal improvement is a prerequisite to leading professionally.**

2

Your attitude is in your control.

THE WORLD SUCKS.

The world is awesome.

Both of these statements are true.

Even in that paradoxical world, *your attitude is in your control.*

We simultaneously live in a world that is the most awesome version of the world so far and the most horrible so far. The former is *more* true than the latter. The world today—at least as I write this, and hopefully still as you read this—does not compare to even the historic everyday horrors of starvation and total abject poverty, let alone global genocides or total wars. But, thanks to the Internet, the world has also gotten smaller, and every day the speed of social media and viral videos leads to new horrors being splashed across our eyeballs and burned into our brains.

The world is *imperfect*, even as, day by day, more people rise out of extreme poverty, and fewer people are enslaved, and freedoms slowly spread around the world, and education access improves. It's easy to lose sight of all of these things, especially if you are near a place where they are *less* true. And every day, your experience is filled with both delights and tragedies, sorrows to rend the soul and joys to lift the heart. How do you deal with that overwhelming emotional experience?

We can choose to not engage in the world, to just put our heads down and pretend that the world today is just as it was every other day in a history we don't carefully look at. On that path lies apathy, but it's a clean and simple apathy, for one simply withdraws a bit from the world, experiencing only one's own private joys and sorrows, except when the world manages to intrude a bit into our isolation.

Or we can choose to be spun up about every outrage, each horror. We can spend our days sharing memes and hot takes on social media and patting ourselves on the back because we spread a little more knowledge of the ill in the world—but at the expense of filling ourselves with anger and spreading that more deeply into our communities. We can be continuously disappointed in our neighbors because obviously they aren't achieving our ideals and assume they must be vile villains bent on destroying the world. We can hate ourselves for our helplessness in the face of that villainy, to see the cost of action being so high that we can never get to it, worn out from the stress of outrage at ourselves and our neighbors.

Or we can choose grace. We can choose to see the good in the world and, beginning with ourselves, amplify that good. We don't need to ignore the bad, but, rather, we counter the darkness with our own light. Not a light of fire and destruction, but a light of peace and joy. It's a harder path, because it is one filled with self-restraint. Like a diet in which we must pass up treats, we must also pass up the rush we get from joining others in righteous anger. We can recognize that we are truly fortunate in ways that most of humanity a century ago couldn't even dream of and use that serenity to weather the troubles that plague our days.

Those are the paths that lie before each of us. The people around us are influenced by the path they see us choose, even as their choice of path influences us. The paths aren't always obvious. Our attitude in looking at the world creates the path ahead of us; we can't always see the path until after we choose it.

> **Your attitude is in your control.**

3

Your blessings exist only if you remember to count them.

A COLLEAGUE OF MINE ONCE ASKED THEIR COWORKERS, "ON A SCALE of one to ten, how fortunate do you feel?" Another colleague immediately said, "Ten. I'm not a nematode."

Think about it. There are, by some estimates, more than a billion insects on the planet for each human. Five hundred fish. Four hundred trees. And that doesn't count bacteria, where we have to use scientific notation just to estimate how many exist. Which means that not only are we a ten on a scale of one to ten, but we're a ten *dozens of times over*! Even on our worst day, we are still much more fortunate than a bacterium floating in the Sargasso Sea.

But let's ignore all of the nonhuman competitors for a moment and marvel at how fortunate we likely are, even among all humans. Baseline quality of life of the median human now is better in so many ways than the quality of life of the most fortunate human one hundred years ago: vaccines, the Internet, better infrastructure. We still have improvements to make, but with more than a hundred billion humans ever born, just being alive *now* rates another ten on a scale of one to ten.

If you're reading this, you likely have other advantages, too, and great blessings. Perhaps you live in a free and prosperous country. Maybe you have a good job and an excellent family. Possibly you're brilliant. You have free time. There are hundreds of ways you can be fortunate, and much of that good fortune doesn't preclude other human beings from *also* being fortunate.

So that's where you start: you are an amazingly blessed individual, even with all that goes wrong in your life. But we get a choice as human beings: we can focus on the good or on the bad. Sadly, all too many humans focus on the bad. We find reasons to be unhappy with our situation, or frustrated at the imperfections of the world, and then we forget to treasure our joys.

Perhaps we are too fortunate. Can a person who has never really seen misfortune grasp how fragile good fortune can be? The people who most seem to optimistically cherish life are the ones with misfortunes that break my heart: the refugee from a war-torn country whose parents were left behind, the parent whose child has a mortal affliction, the veteran who carries hidden scars for life. And the people who have lived a life full of advantage often see the world as irreparably broken—the problems they see feel huge in contrast.

And so each day, I like to think about how fortunate I am. When someone asks me how I am, I've trained my reflexive response to be "I'm fantastic!" It's a reminder to myself to make it true, to see the excellence and grace I am blessed with, and to share it widely. Most people laugh or make a joke—but even in the gentle mockery, they smile, because now they feel a little more fantastic themselves.

My wife started a more specific tradition to count our blessings. Each night at dinner, each family member is prompted to share a bright spot of their day. Even on our worst days, we can show gratitude for something or someone. Remembering that those moments exist helps us build a foundation of serenity.

The reality is that we live in a world so full that, almost by definition, it's a mixed bag of positive and negative situations. Even in a positive or negative situation, it's easy to find elements that run counter. Maybe you got a promotion, but it didn't come with quite the pay raise you expected. Maybe you had a bad encounter with your boss, but a colleague gave you words of encouragement.

The world you live in is just the set of situations that *you choose to focus on*. You can remember all of the bad elements of your day, be convinced that the world is awful and worthless, and respond with frustration and anger. Or you can remember all of the good elements of your day, and be convinced that there is beauty in the world, and respond to nurture and grow that goodness. Your reaction—whatever you choose—then becomes an experience that other people can choose to remember. If you respond to badness with more badness, then you'll increase the net badness in the world near you, which will come back to rebound on you and those around you.

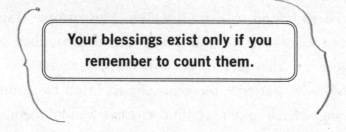

Your blessings exist only if you remember to count them.

4

Becoming right requires accepting that you might be wrong.

YOU ARE WRONG! CONGRATULATIONS!

I know, that seems a little odd. Why am I celebrating being wrong? Because being wrong comes with some amazing superpowers. First, you get the opportunity to learn something new. It's really difficult to learn things when you're already right; it's in acknowledging that we're wrong that we usually get the opportunity to learn new things quickly.

Note that being wrong—or, really, *failing in some way*—isn't a binary condition. You can succeed beyond your wildest imagination and still find errors that you can improve on. Looking for the ways you were wrong and asking, "How could I do this better next time?"

That's the boring superpower. The awesome superpower is that you can't lose an argument when you start out acknowledging being wrong.

That seems weird, doesn't it? Imagine I started a conversation with "The sky is green today." That conversation is . . . not likely to go well. Odds are, anyone I talk to is going to tell me that I'm wrong, that the sky is blue, or gray, or maybe start questioning my choice of pharmaceuticals. Wherever the conversation goes, it's likely to only frustrate me (since whatever reason I had for starting that conversation is something we'll never get to) and anyone else in the conversation (because I'm obviously wrong, so why am I starting pointless arguments), and it's probably a waste of time. But what if, instead, I started out with admitting my own possible error and making a smaller argument?

"I might be wrong, but it seems to me that the sky is a bit green today." How can someone argue with that? By telling me the sky is blue? I've already conceded that point! Instead, I have invited my conversational partner into the real conversation. "Why does the sky seem green to you? What makes you say that?" And now maybe we get into a conversation about the pollen in the sky, or maybe there are cool optical artifacts from the wildfires in California (I'm pretty sure that whenever you're reading this, there are still wildfires in California). But I've invited you past the obvious argument, into a more subtle conversation, and there are only two possible paths: you can quickly agree with me that I'm wrong, in which case I win because not only was I correct in my assessment, but we didn't waste time arguing. Or you can disagree with me (on my wrongness) and tell me I'm right. It's very important to *not* apologize for being wrong at this stage; saying "I'm sorry if I'm being obtuse, but it seems to me that . . ." creates a distracting signal of weakness in many environments.

The value you take away is tied to understanding your objectives in this conversation. Maybe your goal *is* just to be right. That's rarely actually a helpful goal, although you'll encounter many people who seemingly act as if that's their primary goal. But if your goal is to move forward a conversation in a specific direction, then you've played a form of rhetorical jujitsu; your partner gets to be right, *and* you get to have the conversation you wanted.

That later piece is really powerful. A lot of people, when involved in a conversation, want to add value to the conversation. For many people, value comes into being when they make a contribution that they don't think would have been made without their presence. Specifically, they can provide value explicitly by disagreeing with you. "You're not wrong" *is* a form of value that they get to provide.

By starting out with an expression of being wrong, their reflexive disagreement actually furthers the conversation by getting into real agreement. Embrace the possibility of being wrong and move on to being more right more quickly.

> **Becoming right requires accepting
> that you might be wrong.**

5

Even if you don't succeed, a story about failure can be a reward.

NOT EVERYONE LEADS A CHARMED LIFE. I SUSPECT THAT NO ONE leads a charmed life, even those who, when we peer in from the outside as they count their blessings, seem to. For almost everyone, every day includes some event that goes wrong. Not necessarily *horribly* wrong. But, nonetheless, things don't always go according to plan. But when plans fail, you get an opportunity to have an *experience*. And you might learn something.

It was the year 2000, and I'd just started working at Akamai. Despite being a security engineer, I was tagged to audit a software installation, on a distributed network of a few thousand servers around the planet (a number that feels so tiny now, but this was in the precloud era). Our installation process was fairly simple: The installer would "suspend" a group of one-eighth of the machines, which simply told our

16

load-balancing system to stop sending them traffic. Once traffic had been given time to fall off on those machines, the installer would run an installation script that would mass-install all of the systems in the group. Then the auditor would perform a basic checklist on a handful of machines, make sure they seemed all right, and give the installer the go-ahead to start the next group.

You might notice the absence of a command to "unsuspend" any of the machines. In those days, there were two ways to suspend a machine. In one, you sent a signal to the main application on a machine, and it would tell the rest of the network to stop sending it traffic. When that application restarted, it would "forget" that it had been suspended and come back up, ready to serve traffic. Then there was *sticky* suspension, where a configuration file was altered on the machine so that when the application came back up, it would remember to tell the network it was suspended. We used sticky suspension for installs that took multiple steps, like updating the operating system, and regular suspension when we were just updating applications.

That night—we always did installs during US night-time—we were doing a normal software installation. It was my first ever as auditor. The installer was doing his second ever, after doing an operating system upgrade the prior week. They were using the checklist for that installation, which, unfortunately, specified sticky suspension. I, as the auditor, had the checklist for an application installation, which . . . did not.

By the time we were finishing the fifth group and had just suspended the sixth group, the network operations team called me. They had a giant wall of monitors, and every server was displayed by a small rectangle. The rectangle was gray when everything was normal, yellow when machines were suspended, and red when they were down.

"Andy, there are a lot of suspended machines."

"I know, we're doing a software install." And I hung up.

Ring ring. Ring ring.

"No, Andy, there are a *lot* of suspended machines. The whole wall is yellow."

"Uhh . . ." I quickly pulled up our monitoring system. Yup, 75 percent of the network was suspended.

We stopped our install, quickly figured out and solved the issue, and finished up.

This was not an experience I'd qualify as Type 1 fun (fun you have while doing it). It's more like Type 2 fun (fun only in telling the story of its horribleness, like running a marathon). It's easy to take the experience, be upset that it messed up your day (explaining how this had happened to our boss, my colleague getting stuck with the nickname "Sticky"), talk about having a horrible day, and move on.

But in trying to forget about the day, I'd also lose the benefit of the experience. Of learning that human errors result from seemingly simple, but very fragile, complex systems. Of learning not to dismiss a warning from a colleague. Instead, in telling the story, I helped future colleagues see that being the human trigger in a crisis wasn't necessarily career-ending.

Ultimately, in any activity, either you get an experience or you get a story. And you get to choose how you tell the story. And there is something to learn every time your experience isn't perfect.

While the learning is valuable, it's often the story that keeps that learning fresh in our heads; it's the story that allows us to share our experiences with others in relatable ways.

> **Even if you don't succeed, a story about failure can be a reward.**

6

Gift kindness
where it isn't expected.

AS A LONG-TERM EXECUTIVE AT A SUCCESSFUL COMPANY, I RECEIVED
a lot of attempts from vendors to get meetings with me, as
precursors to selling me their product. And by "a lot," that's
generally dozens *every day*. These sometimes come as phone
calls (there's a reason I don't generally answer my phone), but
more often as emails. Most of the time, they're automated,
but many of them are handcrafted; a junior sales representative spent a few minutes looking me up on the Internet and
has been tasked with getting an appointment for me, often
with a more senior sales rep. It's a thankless task, and getting
the deluge of notices can be rage inducing.

I have colleagues across the industry who respond with a
level of snark and condescension, and I've been tempted to,
as well. Usually, I just ignored the messages, even when the

persistent sender kept replying to themselves for the dozenth time.

I was contentedly doing this until a colleague asked me if I'd ever tried telling them no. It seems like such a small thing, but from where I sat it was unnecessary. To the person doing outreach, it would be surprising. It would cost me little and might benefit me (fewer email messages, I hoped). But to the recipient? I would, for a moment, recognize them in a way that few did, and bring a moment of kindness to their day.

So I drafted a template and saved it as a signature file.

Good day!
I'm going to decline what I'm sure was a lovely invitation. I recognize you have a job to do—namely, get a qualified first appointment—but I am not a lead for you, and my answer is no. If I ignored your email, you might reasonably wonder whether I didn't get it, or whether I was considering it. This might reasonably lead to a follow-up. Let me be clear: I received your email and thank you, but I am not interested. Please don't follow up.

I then continued with a brief FAQ listing every objection I could conceive of—and some I missed and added in later—and why that objection wouldn't work for them. I hoped it would make the messages drop off. It did.

But it also resulted in hilarity. I would get replies thanking me for the best message they'd received. I've had people receive the message at multiple companies. It's been shared inside marketing organizations; my own colleagues try to find loopholes. While there are a few people who react with more negative emotions (usually senior executives at very early startups), by and large, this template—which I can use to respond with four mouse clicks—is an act of kindness over and over again, because it's a surprise to most people.

Most of your interactions with other people in the world are, fundamentally, *forgettable*. That may feel unfortunate, in that you aren't leaving a mark in the world. What can be more problematic are the interactions that do stand out. The otherwise forgettable become even more memorable, merely by virtue of standing so alone.

A thoughtless word, a careless error, a social faux pas. Any of these can be a defining moment in the way others in the world view you, because it's all they remember. That memory can easily cast you as a villain for future interactions; even worse, though, that minor harm you accidentally caused causes the other person to look for more negative interactions. Not because they want to, but now because they are sensitized to them. Which, as much as it might harm your reputation, harms them and their outlook on the world even more.

Fortunately, this sword cuts both ways. Unusual interactions stand out, and *kindness* is even more unusual than harm for many people. You have an opportunity to practice random kindness in the world, which both rebounds on you and reflects onto others. Seize that opportunity. But what does it mean to be kind?

For kindness to resonate with its recipient, I think it needs to have a few features. First, and foremost, it must be *unnecessary*. You can't be forced into doing it by the circumstances, or by another person; it must be viewed as a thing you *chose* to do, for no other reason than to be kind.

Kindness must be *joyous*; it must strive to make someone's day better, even if only in a small way.

Kindness must be *unexpected*, a disruption of the routine. Bringing someone flowers once may be kind; delivering them every day may be beautiful, but now it's an expected habit.

Kindness must be *freely given*, without any expectation of recompense or reward. Gratitude is nice, but it mustn't be expected. You give kindness for the sole purpose of improving someone's world, and that improvement is its own reward.

One of the best features of kindness is that in almost every interaction you're having with another person, there is an opportunity to be kind. Kindness can be a small step that simply shows you were trying to improve someone else's day. It's inexpensive and, sadly, still very surprising.

> **Gift kindness where it isn't expected.**

1

Don't borrow evil
where it wasn't intended.

FOR DECADES, BUSINESS AND POP CULTURE HAVE BEEN USING MIL-
itary and combat metaphors—from Sun Tzu's *The Art of War*
and Miyamoto Musashi's *The Book of Five Rings* to analogies
like *defense in depth* and *zero-sum games*—to create models
for resolving interpersonal and interorganizational challenges. This practice, unfortunately, trains us to, by default,
see many of our engagements with others through a narrative lens of conflict: *us versus them*.

Of course, when we tell ourselves the story of our own
life, we generally center ourselves as the hero of the piece.
And if we're a hero, in conflict with another, that person
must be the villain of our narrative. And our goals, when
engaged with a villain, include defeating our enemy, sometimes just because the enemy is there. It's not enough to get
what we want; we also have to beat our opponent.

And that's a problem.

Most of the time, we aren't engaged with a villain. We're engaged with another person, whose goals, skills, and strategies may not perfectly align with ours, but are rarely in direct opposition, either. By treating them as a villain, we create a number of problems for ourselves. We waste a lot of our own energy in the stress of a conflict. We focus on trivialities, just to deprive our opponent of a win, and get distracted from whatever our objectives are. We drive away other people, who try to avoid the negative energy of conflict, both now and in the future. We don't find synergies between our goals where we can combine our energies and both win.

If we can step back for a moment and view the narrative from the point of view of the other person, we might find a similar, but opposite, story. To them, we're the villain and they're the heroine. They're engaged in a conflict with us and also want to win it. And every move we make to stymie them reinforces their assumption that we can't be trusted. When we feel righteously self-justified in treating them poorly, that poor treatment looks exactly like what a villain would do.

It's unpleasant, for us, our counterparty, and any observers. We all carry the negative energy created in unnecessary conflict into future engagements. That inhibits our own performance, the performance of our colleagues, and, frankly, everyone around us.

Rather than treating interactions with people with different goals as hero-versus-villain conflicts, we need to think of ourselves as their sidekick at the moment. How can we help our partner solve the problem they need solved, without unduly sacrificing our needs? Even if our needs are directly in conflict, is there a mutually advantageous compromise that lets us both be happier at low cost? If that sounds hard, imagine two children who want the last piece of cake. They could fight over it, or they could compromise in the time-honored "I cut; you choose" system. That guarantees them both about half a slice of cake, instead of having a fight (after which they discover that an observer ate the cake to put a stop to the conflict—not that that ever happens in our house).

But how do you do it? It's really hard to see the other side of a conflict, especially when you're deeply invested in the argument. Sometimes, it helps to start small.

Like exercising for a triathlon, practicing devillainizing is hard work. Don't start at the capstone, which might be people you disagree with politically. Start with small exercises in devillainization. The easy step is recognizing Fundamental Attribution Error—when you assume (malicious) intent where it doesn't exist. Imagine driving your car and someone slides in front of you. You're mad because that jerk just cut you off!

Feel that anger for a minute. Now pause and rewind. Did you know anything about that driver *before* they pulled in front of you? Probably not, yet now you've judged them, and harshly. You've probably done almost the same thing, without self-reflection. You've pulled in front of other drivers, because you needed to be in that lane. You've waited to put on your signal until it's a fait accompli. Did you do so out of malice? Hopefully not!

Now that you've identified a behavior you do that would piss you off if it was done to you, take this next step. *Every* time you do it—slide in front of another driver—subvocalize, "I bet that annoyed them." Do that over and over again, until when someone pulls in front of you, you're ready to respond. "It's okay. I hope you have a safe drive."

Maybe it isn't driving. Maybe it's aisle blocking in a store. Maybe it's not acknowledging people as they enter a video call. But practice simple acts of charitable courtesy until it's a habit. Think of it as stretching for your triathlon.

Because this part is easy. You're just fighting your modal bias—the preference for the mode you're in, even against modes you use on a regular basis. The next step is much harder: fighting your bias against modes *you don't understand.*

If you're ready for that, now consider when you see someone doing something so startling you wonder, "What were they thinking?" Maybe a sort of "runner-up Darwin Award" activity. Now ask yourself, "What could be true in their world to make this not seem like a horrible idea?"

Humans make middling, marginal decisions all the time. You don't have to assume every choice represents someone's ideal choice. People don't always exercise or eat well. They waste their money on baffling items. They read their texts at an intersection. Those aren't their best available choices—but they aren't always horrible choices.

Practice finding those excuses and beliefs for the people whose decisions you question. That's the whole secret to not villainizing others. Explore what might be true in their world, because we all inhabit different worlds and live different experiences. A choice that may seem kind to you may, in a different context, seem evil to another. When you see a choice that seems poor, finding the charity and grace to see it in its best light removes unneeded stress and conflict from you and the world around you.

> **Don't borrow evil where it wasn't intended.**

8

An uncompelled apology unburdens everyone.

MANY TIMES IN YOUR LIFE, YOU'RE GOING TO HURT SOMEONE. CAUSE someone pain. Hopefully, it will be an unintended harm; you weren't trying to create pain, but you did so anyway. Maybe you were reckless and unaware. Maybe you had to choose between a set of poor choices. The list of ways you might hurt someone is, unfortunately, endless.

The path forward, however, has only a few choices.

There's a choice to ignore the harm. Perhaps you and your victim have a strong relationship, and thus it can survive a little pain. Perhaps you and your victim have no relationship at all, and so the cost of harm doesn't take anything away from the balance sheets of your relationships. A problem with ignoring the harm is that, without communication between both parties, it's a unilateral choice: the perpetrator has decided that the victim can live without recognition of being harmed. Unfortunately, most people aren't just going to forget and move on. The memory of harm will resurface from time to time in similar situations; it's a small poison in their mind, which will haunt all of your future interactions, even if you don't realize it.

There's another choice to offer a pro forma apology. It's an acknowledgment of harm, but without sincerity or accountability. "I'm sorry that you were offended" is a form often seen, when someone is reluctantly apologizing because circumstances require them to, not because they believe they should. They're afraid of appearing weak, but then demonstrate a different sort of weakness by refusing to acknowledge the harm they've caused. The same people who offer pro forma apologies are often the first ones to demand apologies, because apologies are seen as a form of currency, a tribute from the powerless to the powerful. But they couldn't be more incorrect.

An apology is free. The harm has already happened; an apology itself can turn that harm into a benefit, because it signals to the person who was harmed that the harm has resulted in your growth. Imagine if someone commits a minor and small offense against you. It's relatively trivial. You could move on, but, likely, you'll remember it at inopportune moments, even when you're trying to be your best self. And so will the person who wronged you, only more often. They might worry that you're always judging them in that light.

But now, consider an apology. There's a canonical format, established by Lewicki, Polin, and Lount, that defines the six elements of a sincere apology: expressing regret, explaining the failure, acknowledging responsibility, declaring repentance, offering repair, and requesting forgiveness. As a sentence formula, "I am sorry that I took this action that harmed you this way. I wish that I had done otherwise, and in the future, I will do this differently. I can't undo the harm, but can I help by doing this other thing? Can you possibly forgive me?"

The free gift of an uncompelled apology doesn't place you in someone's power; if anything, it *frees* you both from the burden that the error had created. People who are strong in their positions can afford to apologize, because they aren't as worried about the effects of reputational harm. As a manager, I've apologized numerous times to people who work for me, because I make mistakes *all the time*. I didn't give helpful feedback in a timely fashion. I changed the goals of a project midway through because I was incorrect. I made an ill-considered offhand comment. In every case, the apology showed that I wasn't afraid to admit weakness: the offer of a free and sincere apology became a trapping of strength. The more you apologize (within reason!), the stronger you become. In the presence of an honest and unforced apology, the relationship is often stronger.

Apologizing when others are *also* at fault can serve your purposes. Maybe you've asked someone to do something, and they did it poorly—so you can apologize for not being clear. Doing so keeps you both from creating more harm to each other through an argument where you seek to lay blame. Apologizing tells your partner that you really are interested in fixing the interaction, rather than just blaming them. It also creates an opportunity for you to see how reliable your partner will be to you; if they join you in apologizing for their part in the disagreement, you know you have a sincere and honest partner for the future.

Apologies help you find real friends.

Cautionary note: This doesn't mean that you should reflexively say "I'm sorry" whenever you're imperfect, or as a verbal tic, or casually used as a signature is in an email. That's often a defensive reaction developed in response to people who *demand* insincere apologies on a regular basis. If you've developed this pattern as a form of self-preservation, adding honest apologies may not be the right step; instead, reducing the continuous output of apologies could be a better goal. The words "I'm sorry" when not attached to a real apology are often seen as a sign of weakness.

> **An uncompelled apology unburdens everyone.**

9

Regret is an act of forgiveness to your past self.

REMEMBER, FOR A MOMENT, ONE OF YOUR ABSOLUTE WORST moments. The day in which something really bad happened to you, or to someone you loved, and *it was triggered by your poor choice* (I'm not asking you to take blame for something that wasn't your fault, but a moment where, had you done something differently, that day would not have been as awful). Got one?

First, let me extend empathy for the pain you're probably feeling in that memory. It was probably unfair not to warn you that was coming, but how do I even do that? I guess I could tell you to stop reading here, and come back later, starting again, but with foreknowledge. Could I take this moment back and try again? Probably a bad idea. But you've probably sometimes wondered, *what if I could go back and try again?*

And if you've had that thought, you've probably considered all the wonderful ways the time since would be better.

But would it really be? If your moment was truly bad, it was probably world altering, even in a small way. And when you undo that, you undo all of the *good* things that also happened since then. Are there children that never get born? People that never meet? Businesses that don't succeed? Books that never get written? Destroying all of the good since then isn't a positive choice.

What about the lessons you learned? How many times since then have you acted differently than you would have, because you learned something? Maybe you hurt someone, and that hurting has taught you about consequences in a way that makes many of your interactions with people much more positive than they would have been. Or perhaps you lost money after some venture, but the lesson of how you chose poorly has led you to make different risk choices since then.

These "what if" games can trap you in mental loops, exhaust your personal energy, and make it impossible to focus on the future. And for many, that's what regret can feel like. Being trapped in the sin of the past, wishing to undo it as the only way of moving forward. For them, sometimes the only acceptable option is to *not* regret, because then they can move forward without being weighed down by an anchor in the past. Neither of these is a healthy option.

You have made poor choices. You have done things that have harmed people, by intent or by accident. You have hurt yourself.

If you don't learn from those errors, guess what?

You will continue to make poor choices. You will again do things that will harm people, by intent or by accident. You will still hurt yourself.

That seems like an endless hamster wheel of doom, making the same mistakes over and over and never growing as a person. One purpose of life is to grow and become a better human being every day, and that's certainly not a path to it. Regret is the way we learn from our past; it's a form of self-forgiveness. It isn't forgiveness between you and the other person you may have wronged; it's forgiveness between you and the past self who harmed you by making you live with the consequences of your poor choice.

Regret should create a way for you to move forward. You might wish you hadn't done a thing, *but* you did. Learn from whatever mistake you think you made so that you can make better choices in the future, and then *ask yourself for forgiveness*. Giving yourself forgiveness allows you to move forward and work to make the world a better place.

But if you forever play "what if?" games—time traveling in your head, as it were—then you continue to harm yourself. Better to acknowledge that you screwed up, let your past self apologize to your present self, and resolve to do or be better in the future.

> **Regret is an act of forgiveness to your past self.**

10

Stop visiting your Museum of Past Grievances.

I HAD A JOB CANDIDATE WHO, NO MATTER WHAT QUESTION WAS asked of them, would pivot the answer to complain about their current employer. Asked about a time they'd failed, they responded with a litany of why it was the employer's fault. Asked about successes? Everything had happened despite their employer. The amount of negativity they exuded was exceeded only by their lack of self-awareness (it's hard for a prospective employer to see a good relationship with you when all you do is talk about the bad relationship you have). None of their stories sparked joy and triumph; every story they told was full of their grievances. It was easy to pass on someone who advertised that much negativity, especially when I could see the successes they did have in their life. They stand as an obvious cautionary tale—don't be that negative!—but we all bring our own mental negative energy with us from time to time.

Do you have a family member who doesn't seem to know how to give you gifts you'll enjoy? Maybe it's a book you'll never read, so you dutifully express gratitude, and then add it to the shelf you mentally label "books I'll never read." And whenever you're looking for a book, you quickly skip past that shelf, with a negative thought of "why do they keep giving me those books?"

You have a closet full of clothing with logos from an employer who left you with unpleasant memories. You never wear them, but each time you go to pick out a shirt to wear, you recall the anger you felt the day you walked out the door.

You've built a personal Museum of Grievances. These are artifacts, carefully curated, of the people who have done you wrong, and a part of you enjoys the power in the memory—after all, the best vengeance really is living well—and you definitely plan on living well. At the same time, however, your joy is always tainted by the resentment you still feel. Your home or office becomes a monument to the ways you've been harmed in the past, rather than a launching pad into a joyous future.

Just as that candidate carried around a set of negative energy in those mental mementos of their past employers, you've created a physical incarnation to hold all your negative energy, but it's still there right when you least need it. That resentment will build and fester, because you are constantly being reminded of the past. And unlike regret, it isn't a past you can learn from, because you don't see the errors as your own, and revisiting them is unlikely to prompt you to improve your own behavior. Instead, revisiting the errors of others makes it easier for you to tell the story of how *they* were the villain, and that reinforced belief will cloud any future interaction you have with them.

Even if you're not quite to the minimalist phase of throwing out the things that don't bring you joy, perhaps you can pack them away. Take the mementos that bring out that distress and box them away. Scatter those books you aren't likely to read into different bookcases (even better if those bookcases belong to someone else). But take away that fresh and daily reminder of even a minor grievance. The opposite of hate isn't love; it's indifference. Become indifferent by refusing to be reminded of petty negatives from your past.

Because who wants to visit a museum dedicated to negativity? And if you wouldn't want to visit one, why do you live in one?

Stop visiting your Museum of Past Grievances.

11

The only thing keeping you from having more fun than you are having right now is you.

MY FIFTIETH BIRTHDAY FELL TWO YEARS INTO COVID. IT HAPPENED to be in the middle of a sales off-site for an employer I'd joined during the pandemic. So I treated that day as the extended birthday party I couldn't have, even dancing in the rain in Miami when the evening cocktail party was inundated by a passing squall. A colleague who had worked with me at a previous employer told me he'd never seen that side of me. I suspect part of that was that I was always concerned about my image with our previous employer, but at our current one, I had realized that it didn't matter nearly as much. But a bigger factor was that, along the way, I had learned how to have more enjoyment in life. The lesson came, of all places, from my own children.

"Dad, let's walk on the wall!" I think any parent of a small child has had this moment. You're walking down the street, with your just-mastered-not-falling-down child, and now they want to do something outrageous. In public. In front of everyone. You'd rather not. Decades of adulthood, coming on the awkward heels of being a teenager, have taught you not to stand out by being silly. How do you possibly get out of this moment?

The reality is that you probably *don't really have a choice.* As a parent, you'll often have to disappoint your children as you teach them the rules of life, but you also need to *not* disappoint them out of spontaneous joy for no good reason. Walk on that wall, sing and laugh and dance like a fool, and, most important, *have fun.* Dance like nobody's watching, even though you know everyone is. And while you might be embarrassed at first, you'll grow past it.

The best shield against the shame of public displays of enjoyment is a small child. You can have fun with them in ways you'd be mortified if you were doing it solo, until you realize a truth of the universe: the only thing keeping you from having more fun than you are having right now is you. You get in your own way. You worry about what other people will think of you, and how you'll embarrass yourself, and you *stop having fun.*

As adults, we are often faced with pressure—some real, some imaginary—to conform to some notion of professional, boring behavior. Some of those rules *are* important, but many of them aren't. When you're on business travel, and your employer is picking up the tab, you shouldn't do anything but work. When you're in the office, you must wear boring clothes.

Perhaps you have a persona you wear around as a serious professional, and you wouldn't think of relaxing that in front of work colleagues. In some circumstances, that rule might be critical to your job progression, but it isn't always.

If a rule *isn't* relevant, examine if it is inhibiting joy. Perhaps you enjoy brightly colored socks or a hand-knitted shawl to spice up your outfit. That bit of joy you wear for yourself brings joy to others, as well; it can also create a moment of connection when you find someone else who appreciates you. When you travel, do you try new foods or just eat safe things? This is a tension for me, since dietary restrictions can make new foods dangerously *unsafe*, but there is a pleasure in eating something you've never had before and may never have again.

Do you turn down a colleague or a friend when they invite you to a new activity, because you've never done it before and you'll probably embarrass yourself with how bad at it you'll be? If you don't care about how bad you are, *neither will anyone else*. But your enjoyment at trying, at sometimes failing, is available to you only if you seize the opportunity.

Because tomorrow, that wall might not be there to walk on. Enjoy your blessings when they're present. If you're not having more fun, make sure there is a good reason for it.

> **The only thing keeping you from having more fun than you are having right now is you.**

12

Make expensive time worth it.

I'm going to bring a football home for you.
—LOGAN RYAN

No, bring two. One for me and one for Ozzy.
—ASHLEY RYAN

ON NOVEMBER 2, 2020, ASHLEY RYAN ALMOST DIED.

Over a thousand miles away from her husband and children, an ectopic pregnancy almost claimed her life; only thanks to the advice of one of her husband's trainers, Justin Maher, did she go to the emergency room for lifesaving surgery. Six days later, her husband suited up for the New York Giants.

It would be easy to glimpse only those facts and spin a narrative of a husband focused on his career, leaving his wife to suffer alone. But that's not the case here. Ashley was stable the next morning; despite the support of Joe Judge, the Giants' head coach, who told Logan to head to his wife and family and take what time was needed, *Ashley* is the one who decided that Logan should stay and play, that his sacrifice and dedication to football the prior year should not be discarded.

But she gave him one request. To bring a pair of balls home. And he did. A forced fumble early on, and, as the game wound down, Logan iced the game with an interception, sealing a victory for his team.

Most of us aren't NFL players, let alone great NFL players. And hopefully, most of us won't have to go through an ectopic pregnancy. But all of us have periods of time where we have paid a high emotional cost for a brief window of time. When *we* pay the cost, it's easy for us to maximize our enjoyment; if we consume limited vacation time to travel, of course we want to enjoy it! But it's much harder when someone else—especially someone we love—is paying the cost for us.

Perhaps it's business travel and you have small kids at home. Your spouse is now juggling parenting alone, along with whatever else they were doing, and you feel guilty for having any fun. But adding your misery at being far away to their misery at paying the cost for you isn't going to make the world any better for anyone.

You've already paid the cost. Now maximize the value. If you're on business travel, do one outlandish tourist thing. I like to do the things that my wife would do if she were there, even if I think they're less fun. I'm afraid of heights, but she enjoys climbing mountains. So one trip, I climbed the bridge in Sydney Harbor. I'm not a fan of cold water, but she swims until her feet are blue. If I'm ever staying in a hotel on a beach (usually off-season, because that's how industry conferences tend to roll), I go for a swim. I'll even make a short video to send to her (short because, well, brrrr), so she can enjoy the vicarious experience.

I bring back keepsakes to remember those awesome moments, which fit into trips that we'd already paid high value for, because our shared goal is to create great memories, even in moments of trial.

While for some, suffering is alleviated by seeing others suffer, in general, that creates a reinforcing downward spiral—when does it become acceptable to *stop* suffering? Instead, find the place when you've already paid the price to create a return that brings joy together.

Just make sure that, in any relationship, the price isn't always paid by the same person. A useful test? Each of you should have days where you're pretty sure the other one has the better side of the deal and days where you know you have the better end. Just don't count them too closely. But when you have the better end of the deal, make sure you maximize how much value you can get.

> **Make expensive time worth it.**

13

Your wellness is one of the greatest assets you control.

Be sure to secure your own mask
before assisting others.
—PREFLIGHT SAFETY BRIEFING

IT'S TWO THIRTY IN THE MORNING, AND YOUR PHONE RINGS. IT'S A work emergency, and you've got to solve it. You're back in bed by four, only to get back up at six, get your day started, and head in to work. You make sure to drink some extra coffee, perhaps, but, nonetheless, you're working in a bit of a haze all day long. By the time you head home, you aren't sure what day of the week it is anymore, and you probably don't really remember the last few hours as being productive.

The cause of your foggy day might vary. Perhaps you're recovering from a head cold, or suffering from seasonal allergies, or you were taking care of a family member the night before. Maybe you were just up late watching your favorite sports team winning a championship. The reasons might change, but, ultimately, when it comes to prioritizing between taking care of our health, or showing up to work, we rarely prioritize our own health. For many, that even extends to choices between their own health and helping take care of family members.

Prioritization is *hard*. Perhaps we need to prioritize two activities, A and B. We often think that "A is more important than B" means that "Don't do B until A is done," when we really mean, "B shouldn't get all of our energy and starve A." Usually, we need to do *both* A and B, and maybe one has more flexible time constraints than the other one does.

Consider *exercise* and *going to work*. Obviously, going to work is a must-do activity, but is it really more important to you than staying healthy? It's hard to see a case for "don't bother exercising at all," even if you're not about to embark on a hard-core routine reminiscent of boot camp. Conversely, there is rarely an argument for "don't bother going to work *at all*," just to make space for exercise. But all too often, work not only takes precedence over exercise, but completely replaces it.

Your wellness is one of the single greatest assets you control. With wellness, you increase not only your own quality of life, but also your career productivity. Wellness ought to be your *highest* priority, although for too many people it ends up becoming the *lowest* priority. Prioritizing your wellness has both a strategic prong and a tactical one.

Strategically, you ought to have a plan for your wellness. I'm not a lifestyle coach, and I'm not going to give you a specific plan, but it ought to involve not only physical elements like health maintenance, fitness, nutrition, and sleep, but also mental and emotional elements as well. Build your long-term plan, appropriate to your body's needs, so that you can also make wise tactical choices.

Tactically, on many days you will be faced with wellness trade-offs. You need to recognize that you *are* making choices, and then decide if those are really the choices you want to make. Do you stay up late to watch a football game? Go drinking with friends on a weeknight? Go to work when you've got a mild head cold (which is also making a wellness choice for *all of your coworkers*)? Stay in the office even though you're just staring at a monitor, getting more stressed because you're neither productive nor resting?

Your wellness is in your hands. You're going to have to make hard choices, and not all of them will be ones you will like. But when you start to recognize that wellness is an asset, you can start to make maintenance and improvement investments in it just as you might for any other asset.

Wellness also requires that you set boundaries and stick to them. In some environments, boundaries aren't well-respected, *especially* if they are explained. Some will try to "help" you balance by finding ways to move your boundaries. In those cases, it can be better to shift from specific, descriptive explanations of your boundaries ("I can't work late that evening because I'm going out to dinner with my spouse") to more generic ones ("Unfortunately, I have a difficult-to-reschedule appointment then").

One boundary that is relatively easy to set is around vacation boundaries. Many people find that the first day back from vacation is stressful, because you're trying to juggle catching up on email, along with the regularly scheduled meetings and the escalations that people held until you were back. One common defense mechanism is to spend the last day of your vacation reading email.

Don't do this. You'll resent your employer and your colleagues, and you'll wipe out the wellness benefits of the vacation almost immediately. Instead, block your calendar for a *pretend* vacation day at the end of your vacation. Tell your distant colleagues you'll be out that extra day. Don't take meetings. You'll still be working, but reading your email. If you're a manager, delegate to someone to keep track of important things while you're away, and use that list to prioritize the work you'll look forward to.

Make your plans for the next few days based on changing priorities. If you have spare time, use it to catch up on a project that relies on you. But don't let your energy be drained on that first day back—you'll appreciate it, your colleagues will appreciate it, and your employer will appreciate it. But no one is going to do this for you; you have to do it for yourself.

But until others start looking out for your wellness, you'll need to take care of your own first. And then you can start helping your colleagues with their wellness.

> **Your wellness is one of the greatest assets you control.**

14

Retain the confidence of the new learner, and temper it with the caution of the old hand.

IT WAS A LOVELY DAY ON KAUAI WHEN I HEADED OUT FOR A RUN. I'D been running at that point for about a year and could reliably pull off a 5K with a lot of sweat. We were staying just a short walk from the beach, and as my run took me past the beach, I pondered how triathletes must do it. Could I? I was wearing my Vibram FiveFingers and triathlon shorts, so I could totally do the water. I dropped my T-shirt on a rock, ran out into the water, and started to swim.

The beach I swam out from was less than a quarter mile from the beach I thought I'd swim over to. How hard could that be? But when I realized I needed to abort about halfway through my swim—the waves were tough—there was only a rocky shoreline I could head for. A pair of skinned and banged-up knees later, I was out of the water and slunk over to recover my shirt, hoping no one had noticed.

The Darwin Awards are a celebration of some of humanity's finest examples of *overconfidence bias*: a belief that your capabilities are much greater than they are. Overconfidence bias often shows up most obviously when people are barely skilled in an area; people with greater skill might be overconfident, but it's a little harder to detect.

It always feels easier to identify someone else's overconfidence than our own. We see a colleague giving a presentation when we know that they just learned the material yesterday. We hear them answer a question, and we're pretty sure they just made up the answer.

On the flip side, there are times when rather than feeling overconfident, you question whether you even belong. You look around, and everyone else projects their own confidence (or is it overconfidence?), and you wonder if you even belong in their presence. You start a new job, and everyone around you seems better qualified than you are. You're in the middle of your career, and you're called in to be the expert advising people far senior to you. Even when others see you at the peak, you still feel underqualified to be in the room.

Impostor syndrome is that feeling. You *know* you absolutely don't belong, and your anxiety that you'll be caught out and discovered makes it hard for you to function. Perhaps you're extra careful about making mistakes—and the easiest way to not make mistakes is to not do anything.

Some of these effects are an observation problem. You suffer impostor syndrome because you don't see your own capabilities in the same light as others see them . . . and overconfidence is just the same, but in the opposite direction. Sometimes they are induced by others. You suffer from overconfidence because no one has ever directed criticism at you, . . . or you suffer impostor syndrome because you've received a never-ending stream of critical feedback.

Both of these are real effects. We often feel empathy for those who suffer impostor syndrome and disdain for people who exhibit overconfidence, but the reality is that growth comes most readily if you realize that you can skate on the boundary of the two and draw a little bit from each.

Overconfidence allows us to take risks that aren't proportional. We discover things that we can do, despite the lack of any historical evidence that we ought to be able to do them. We learn from our failures, in ways that we wouldn't have if we didn't try. If we take just a little bit of overconfidence, we can stretch ourselves in surprising ways. That not-so-wise attempted swim in Kauai? Seven years later, I ran my first triathlon, raising thousands of dollars for charity. It took overconfidence multiple times to get me over the failures that would have inhibited me.

Impostor syndrome amplifies those failures in our own minds. We replay them over and over, because we worry that we won't get another chance at failure, and so we are spurred to learn the most we can from any mistake we do make. If we take just a little bit of being an impostor, we can maximize how much we learn from our attempts. We may need to practice forgiving ourselves for those failures, but we must also practice learning from them.

> **Retain the confidence of the new learner,
> and temper it with the caution of the old hand.**

15

To engage in the present, be of two minds about the future.

FEBRUARY 5, 2017, HOUSTON, TEXAS. THE ANNUAL CLIMACTIC GAME of the NFL season was taking place, and the New England Patriots had fallen behind the Atlanta Falcons 28–3 in Super Bowl LI. For all intents and purposes, the game was *over* in the third quarter. And I was there, accompanied by our two preteen children.

My daughter, the diehard football fan, had been miserably sick the day before and was slumped in her seat, too low energy to do more than observe. My son had inherited the energy of the crowd—as heartsick as my daughter was actually sick—and was also slumped in his seat. The fans all around us in the stadium were morosely looking around, perhaps wondering if they could make a quick exit out of the stadium.

I recalled a conversation I'd had at another football game almost four years earlier with Ed Solder, father to the Patriots' starting left tackle, Nate Solder. At halftime, the Patriots were down twenty-four to *zero* against the Peyton Manning–led Broncos. I knew how hard this was as a fan, but I couldn't imagine how hard it was as a parent. The Solder family sat about ten rows behind us, and, when we'd both gone up to get out of the bitter cold of the day, I pulled out a cocktail-party trick I learned a long time ago. "Ed," I said, "I know how hard this is as a fan, but I can't imagine how difficult this is as a parent. How do you handle it?" (The cocktail-party trick is this: Ask someone what they do with their time, and then respond, "Wow, that sounds really challenging. How do you deal with . . ." and pick some feature of their vocation that seems hard.)

"Well," he replied, "you don't really expect them to win. But you go out and root for them to at least put together one good drive, and maybe score a touchdown. As long as Nate is out there playing, I'll be out cheering him on." That game, of course, is really memorable not just for my recollection of Ed's words, but because the Patriots came from behind to win 34–31 in overtime.

I recalled those words, sitting in the stands at Super Bowl LI, considering how I would give encouragement to my own kids. And, if we're being honest, to myself. I've found a great way to improve my own outlook is to help other people improve theirs. But Ed's wisdom, while helpful to me about just taking the next step, wouldn't, I think, resonate. The anxiety of preteens is a little different from the sadness of an adult.

While I considered, the Patriots had finally scored a touchdown, but missed the point after. At 28–9, the Patriots needed, in just over seventeen minutes of game time, a field goal and two touchdowns, just to tie. And those touchdowns both required two-point conversions. It was dire, and my kids had wilted a bit more.

"Look," I said, "you have to live in two different worlds right now. In one of those worlds, the Patriots have already lost this game, and we still have to experience the last ninety minutes or so. But really, it's just a football game. We've had a great weekend, and sure, we'll be sad we don't get to taunt people with another Super Bowl victory, but really, it isn't going to get any worse for us. Just process that loss *right now* and move on. But in the other world, the Patriots are going to come from behind. And it'll be epic. And we were here for it. But to help make that happen, we're going to need to do our jobs and be loud. And when they win, we'll know we were part of it. But if they lose, we can pretend that ninety minutes was just fun, because we've already processed our sadness about their loss. So let's do this." And I stood up.

"But Dad," my son said, "everyone else is sitting down."

"Not for long." And, like that one fan often made fun of in sports commercials, I raised my voice. "Let's go! DEFENSE! Get on your feet! One more!" There might have, um, been some profanity in those statements.

Behind me, a gentleman said, "Um, they need three scores, not one."

To which I responded, loudly, "And how do you count to three? First you need one. Now GET ON YOUR FEET!"

And he did. And then another. And then the two sections around us rose with a wave and a roar, and right in front of us an Atlanta offensive lineman committed a holding penalty (I like to think that we helped him do that). And half a quarter later, again right in front of our loud screaming section, Dont'a Hightower decided he wanted the ball, and he went and got it. I don't think he needed our help for that one, but it was fun to watch the play—and the end result of the game, as the Patriots took the game to overtime and won, 34–28.

And we had no stress at that point, because we'd already accepted the bad consequences in our hearts and had moved on to the positives. We weren't worried about the loss, because that loss already existed in the other world. So we got to fully and completely enjoy the experience in a way that we wouldn't have if we hadn't been able to embrace the negative and the positive at the same time.

It's the fear of the negative outcomes that often cripples our decision-making process and adds stress to our choices. "What if this goes bad?" we ask ourselves, but then we don't answer the question. The answer is, "So what if it does? Am I prepared to accept that possibility?" If so, I can have the serenity to accept it, and enjoy the possible, without the stress hanging over my head.

If those positive possibilities come true, and you achieve your success—material wealth, a championship, life goals—those are worth celebrating. But failure to achieve those possibilities ought not lessen your sense of self-worth or destroy your worldview. But the anxiety that keeps you from trying for those successes simply because failure is too terrifying? That can be crippling.

We're sometimes afraid to process a loss earlier than we need to, because then we risk having to experience it twice, once in anticipation and once when it happens. But if we can anticipate all of the outcomes—living in two worlds, as it were—we have to experience the *shock* of the negative outcome only once. And the part of our mind that is considering the positive outcome does not have to carry the negative anticipation anymore, because the *other part of our mind* is doing so.

Having two minds and experiencing two different future worlds allows us to persevere even in the face of almost certain disaster.

> **To engage in the present,
> be of two minds about the future.**

16

Practice the future
to face adversity with grace.

ARE YOU AFRAID OF SOMETHING? BEING FIRED FROM YOUR JOB? Being turned down for an opportunity? Being spurned by someone? Any of these fears can get in our way. Worrying about the future is a normal reaction, but that worry can sometimes prevent us from making plans. Worse, we often don't even plan for the things that most worry us.

Imagine for a moment that you're being fired or laid off. You arrive for a one-on-one meeting with your manager, and . . . there's an HR professional in the room. They ask you to sit down, and you do. Your heart is already racing. Did you do something wrong? Can you change the outcome of this meeting? What are you going to do?

They inform you that the company has decided to go in a different direction, and your services are no longer required. Do you plead to keep your job? Are you angry at the foolishness of this choice—you're irreplaceable!—and do you start an argument with your boss?

Let that conversation play out in your head.

Pause for a moment. If this is your first time ever doing this mental exercise, you're probably a bit distressed right now, *especially* if you have been let go from a company before. Your anxiety might have gone up, because *you've just been fired*. Playing it out in your head feels like the real thing, so take a moment if you need one (don't worry, these words will still be here if you need to walk away for a bit).

You've now made it part of your reality, and that often makes people more nervous about the encounter. You've already felt the pain, and now you don't want to feel it again. Sure, you've eliminated a little bit of the surprise of the pain, but that alone won't help very much. It's natural to not want to play this scenario out again, but planning for the future requires you to overcome this moment.

Repeat this exercise a few more times. Each time, you're going to pretend you react differently. Outrageously, even. Let yourself mentally pound the table. Say something you'd never say in real life. Do this until you get a little bored with the conversation. The *entire* purpose of this exercise is to eliminate your surprise, because the goal is to plan for your action. Have you ever seen a car collision or other minor disaster? Did you notice how many people just stood there, doing nothing for a few moments? This is known as the *bystander effect*, and it is amplified both by the number of people also standing around as well as by the absence of a trained plan. And many people, when they do act, act with panic, sometimes doing more harm than good.

This is why emergency responders *practice* scenarios, so they don't give in to panic. But no one ever teaches you to be your own emergency responder for the unpleasant events in your life. You aren't practicing these events to make yourself worried about the future; you're practicing until you're no longer worried about that unpleasant future, because you know how to handle it now.

You can start to build scenarios in your head for *how* you can better handle the encounter, but there's really one important question to ask yourself:

Are you proud of your behavior?

Consider being let go from your employer. That meeting already had a fixed script. Nothing you will say or do is going to result in any changes to the outcome. You're being let go. But did you take the news with dignity? If not, do it again, and again, until you are proud of your reaction. This is the same skill you use in preparing for crises: practice the future, until the reaction is one that you can execute without panic.

You won't always guess the surprise correctly—maybe that meeting is a fact-finding inquiry about another employee's behavior—but the calmness that you'll call on in dealing with the surprise will still be a useful tool. And others will observe the professional manner in which you dealt with surprising adversity.

Choose a manner that makes you proud. Planning for improbable adverse events allows you to act how you would want yourself to, even if it is a surprise.

> **Practice the future
> to face adversity with grace.**

17

Helping others is an investment in helping yourself.

EVERYBODY HAS BAD DAYS. *ASKING* **FOR HELP IS, FOR MANY, A CHAL-**lenge, not least because we're afraid of rejection. We might not get the help we asked for, it might feel forced or inauthentic, or what we asked for isn't really what we need. Sometimes, it's hard to even see a way to help ourselves, and if we can't see how others could help us, how could we ask another to help us in a way we don't understand?

At that moment when you can't see a path to getting help yourself, sometimes it's better to back away from a focus on helping yourself. Because when you fail (and, if you disbelieve you can help yourself, you are more likely to fail), you'll often be worse off than you were before, because not only did you have a bad day, but now you're a failure on top of it, at the one thing that mattered most to you.

But there is still a path to help yourself.

In the words of Fred Rogers, "When I was a boy and I would see scary things in the news, my mother would say to me, 'Look for the helpers. You will always find people who are helping.'" It's not just the bystanders who are improved by helpers; both the person helped and the helper themselves see benefit. So, when you're having a rough patch, it can be a useful strategy.

Try to help someone else. Anyone else. In fact, find someone as far away in your network as possible, and give them a gift of joy. Why? First, you distract yourself from your own problem; that creates distance that is helpful for restoration. Second, you are improving the world for someone else; that's a worthwhile goal in and of itself, and you know it, and that will improve your outlook. Third—and this is both important and serendipitous—the act of giving joy creates or strengthens a connection, and often joy reflects back at you. And finally, you can succeed at something. And that success might give you the confidence to act in a way to help yourself.

As she recounts to her @saysthefox Twitter followers, at the start of the 2020 coronavirus pandemic, photographer Kelly Victoria found herself out walking late at night to process some painful personal challenges. She came across a fairy garden in her neighborhood, created by a four-year-old who wanted to "spread some cheer" as her own antidote to loneliness (kudos to her and her parents for this idea). Victoria left a note, pretending to be the fairy that lived in the tree, and for the next nine months, the two exchanged notes and gifts, brightening each other's lives in a way neither could have anticipated when they each took their first steps toward brightening someone else's day.

Each one, while feeling their own pain, felt joy in helping someone else out. Each made a fantastic friend and helped themselves by focusing on helping someone else. Neither had an expectation, other than that they might bring someone a smile for one day.

But at the same time, neither one actually *knew* the depth of the other's needs. In a traditional "scary situation" (like a fire or accident), the need is blatant and obvious, and one needs merely overcome the bystander effect to find a way to help. But there exist many ways to help that aren't in acute crisis situations, and those are often the little opportunities that can help us as we help others.

When you most need emotional help, you can find it by giving it to others.

> **Helping others is an investment
> in helping yourself.**

18

Serenity is knowing that the crap you're wading through is crap you chose to deal with.

THERE'S AN OLD JOKE THAT I FIRST HEARD FROM MY PARENTS—AND I suspect that might be the norm, as what makes it funny is hearing your parents say a naughty word—about a man and a mule wandering through the desert. As the storyteller tells the joke, describing the environment, they frequently interrupt themselves, as the mule asks for water, to which the man always replies, "Patience, jackass, patience."

As the story goes on, the desert scene unfolds, with descriptions becoming more and more outlandish yet simultaneously plebeian. Because there is no end to the joke. The gag is to get one of the listeners to ask *when we'll get to the punch line*, to which the storyteller replies, "Patience, jackass, patience."

Serenity is the opposite of stress. Stress is the feeling you get when your expectations of the world don't match what the world is actually providing. For the audience of the joke, they *expected* a punch line of the joke, and, not getting one, stress drives them to act. That reaction is the straight line that the comedian needed for their punch line.

But sometimes, we aren't waiting for a punch line. Life does, sometimes, throw us surprising curveballs, but often, the unpleasantness we encounter every day is entirely predictable. Maybe we have to wake up earlier than we'd like to get our kids to school—or to hop onto a work meeting because we took an offer with a company a few time zones to the east.

Maybe we're driving change in our company, and every day is full of copies of the same meeting, as we meet with every stakeholder and struggle to get the flywheel of change moving. And it might feel like that flywheel has barely started. So we feel stress, as we look around ourselves at the situation, and think, *This can't be right*. At one level, that's a fine outlook—we shouldn't just accept a poor situation—but on another level, it's problematic for us.

We expect the world to be an easy place, but we've chosen to be in a situation where it isn't. To achieve our goals, we've moved out of our comfort zone, because we hope to get to a better place on the other side. Now we have increased our stress levels, because the world isn't meeting our expectations.

But the world is never an easy place.

The trick to serenity—the ability to endure patience without stress—requires intentionality. *Because* you've decided you're willing to pay the cost to improve your world, and now you have *chosen* to pay that cost, the cost becomes more bearable. It might be that you've merely chosen to pay a lesser cost; rather than change the world, you're changing your interaction and refusing to let the world run you over emotionally. But in recognizing that you've chosen to pay the cost, you've changed your expectation of the world.

And in choosing to pay the cost, you've taken control of your own emotional health. And that's a place where serenity comes from: the wisdom to accept that the cost you're paying isn't a cost that you are willing to change and that your world is exactly as difficult as you expect it to be.

For now.

> **Serenity is knowing that the crap you're wading through is crap you chose to deal with.**

Notes for Part I:
Personal Leadership

HAVING MADE IT THIS FAR, BEFORE YOU DIVE INTO THE NEXT SECTION, take a moment for some reflection. Divide up the chapters into the following categories, and then engage with them accordingly going forward. If you need a chapter list as a reference, the Appendix has the chapter titles with brief summaries, and the Contents simply has the chapter titles.

- Which lessons immediately resonated with you as skills that you already practice? These are your advanced skills. They're great to have, and maybe you should check back every once in a while to make sure you aren't misusing them. But when do they not work for you? Are those opportunities for you to practice that skill or challenges to use a different approach? Learning the difference between those two paths makes it easier to guide others who are working on their skills.

- Which lessons can you see how to apply, but still need practice? They aren't yet second nature. Look back each week to spot opportunities where you could have used them . . . and try to use them next week. Every week, practice them until you use those skills without even thinking about it.

- Are there any lessons that fell flat, because you've already tried those skills, but they didn't work for you? Fantastic! At least one of us is wrong, which means there is an opportunity for learning here. What would have to be true in your world for that skill to be useful? Is that a change you can make, or do you need outside help to do so? Or maybe I was wrong—find my contact information in the back of the book and help me see what I'm missing, so I can give better advice going forward.

- Do any lessons seem applicable to other people, but not to yourself? Odds are, you've got a big blind spot (maybe not, but run with it for a moment). Do you have a friend or colleague whom you trust and who trusts you? Ask them for advice. Maybe there is something you're missing. If you don't have someone, try this exercise: every time you think this lesson would apply to someone else, tell yourself what they did that made you believe that. After a while, you'll notice a pattern. Some set of actions makes you think this skill is useful. Now start watching your own behavior, and look to see when you take those actions.

PART II

TEAM LEADERSHIP

NOW THAT YOU'VE LEARNED TO LEAD YOURSELF—OR MAYBE YOU skipped that section and will go back to it later—it's time to apply the next level of skills: leading the team around you. This section focuses on lessons that you'll use in directly interacting with other people. Those people might work for you, or you might work for them. Maybe they are peers. Perhaps they are colleagues in a far-off part of the organization. Some of these lessons work better when you have the authority to implement them. Others work well through influence or through modeling a behavior. But in every case, these lessons are about how you directly lead the people around you, through your own interactions with them.

These lessons are about interpersonal interactions, not organizational dynamics. In the same way that skills you practiced in "Personal Leadership" are skills that others around you can also use, the skills you will develop here are also useful to the members of your team in working with others around them.

Great leaders make their teams feel seen in every interaction. It can be a small touch, but people come to want to be in your vicinity because they see that you act with care, rather than indifference.

19

Leadership is helping someone become a better version of themselves.

I'VE BEEN LECTURED TO ABOUT LEADERSHIP MORE TIMES IN MY LIFE than I can shake a stick at. I've heard different definitions of leadership, from "Getting people to do something they wouldn't otherwise do," which, honestly, sounds more like a used-car salesperson than an infantry officer taking a hill. Maybe it's "Inspiring someone to be part of something greater than themselves," which might sound a bit like a religious prophet. Sometimes it's about having a vision for the future or getting more out of the people you lead.

What I've generally encountered is that common depictions of leadership—at least the ones I've been exposed to, often taught by academics in small classrooms, far away from the troubles of reality—all seem to revolve around leadership as a way to turn people into tools. In practice, they often talk about *followership* as a component of *leadership*, as if there is a hierarchy where we all follow the leader above us, in a chain leading up to some Supreme Leader somewhere.

Sounds scary. This treats leadership as a tool, a weapon to be used in that hierarchy, and leadership flowing from one leader to the next. One bad leader in that chain creates mistrust for all of the leaders around them. People will shy away from following leaders that they do not trust. Bad leaders will inhibit growth and development if people believe the leader is using that development as a weapon against their best interests.

I believe that leadership is a form of service, of stewardship. When you lead people, it isn't about the ways in which you might use them for your purposes; leadership is about helping someone become a better version of themselves. You may get to lead them for a day, a decade, or a lifetime, but you are merely a steward of their time with you, and leadership means that you are going to give them the space to grow, develop, and, someday, leave your care.

Along the way, you *might* directly gain net benefit from their development. Certainly, if you're a manager, you hope so. After all, you're paying them to do work for you! But management isn't the only form of leadership, just the *easiest*. It's the easiest because you have support structures, and norms, and, most important, either of you can end the relationship pretty easily.

Parenting is also a form of leadership. Almost all the advice that follows applies to parents, maybe with a slight twist: parents don't get to fire their children, even if most of us have considered it a time or two (in fairness, I'm pretty sure my kids ponder the inverse far more often). Teaching is a form of leadership. So is health care. So is having a conversation in a coffee shop or on an airplane. Sometimes it's more obvious that you're in a leadership role, but almost anytime you get the opportunity to interact with a human, you have an opportunity to help them become a better version of themselves.

Whether you choose to take it is up to you.

Leadership also carries a responsibility. When you're helping someone to grow, you need to create a safer environment for them to do so. They might be swimming in shark-infested waters, and you have the responsibility to fence off a lagoon for them to operate in. But a universal way to create a safe place is to visibly model the actions you expect of them. Are you teaching people how to take care of themselves? Then they need to see you taking care of yourself, or else they won't believe it is safe to do so. They have to observe you praising others for doing so, to come to believe that you mean it.

Most important, leadership is *also* about you and your own self, even while setting aside your ego. Every action you take as a leader reflects on every other action you take and everything you say. Effective leadership requires careful authenticity, because one ill-spoken phrase can counter the effects of years of good work. It's about understanding how your actions will change the world, rather than understanding how you are more *right* in a given moment. Because sometimes, being *right* deprives you of the opportunity to *lead* someone.

I was once trying to describe the dangers of a risk in one of our systems to other managers, and I clearly wasn't getting through. In an effort to make it more visible, I said, "How would you feel if it was *your* information that was exposed by this?"

The room went silent. Many sets of eyes looked at me until I became uncomfortable, and I moved on, not understanding why that tactic hadn't worked. Afterward, my boss met with me and told me that it had sounded like a threat, and what was I trying to accomplish? When I said I just wanted action, he replied, "Before you open your mouth, know what you're trying to achieve." *Action* isn't a goal; it's just chaos. Leadership isn't about generating action; it's about improving the world by helping other people improve the world.

On that day, I failed at leadership, but it taught me a lesson that I'll never forget. There are a lot of ways to lead people, but they all require that you know what you're trying to achieve. One goal is to create an environment where it is easier for people to grow than it was for you to grow.

> **Leadership is helping someone become a better version of themselves.**

20

Inclusion is reducing the energy cost someone has to pay just to exist in a space.

THIS ISN'T YET ABOUT *PROFESSIONAL INCLUSION*, ABOUT MAKING sure that someone's *ideas* are being included. There's a reason for that. If you don't first address *personal inclusion*, about making the human feel welcome in a space, then efforts at professional inclusion are going to be less effective and can even be damaging.

When people aren't included, they're encountering friction just engaging in apparently normal interactions. That friction burns the energy and mental focus they need to excel at life. It even makes them feel not included at times when they otherwise wouldn't notice. Sometimes, that friction shows up in really big and painful ways, but most of the time, it shows up in small ways. It makes them feel like an outsider, an "other" (and hence the verb form, "othering").

For some examples, let's take a look at the day of a hypothetical person, Taylor.

Well, Taylor's day starts the night before. Taylor's boss needed to schedule a meeting urgently, but didn't want to rearrange their own calendar, and the only free slot was at 8:00 a.m. Unfortunately, Taylor has kids to get out of the house in the morning, so Taylor can't quite get out of the house in time to make that meeting normally. Taylor has to choose: Be seen as a complainer and say you can't make the meeting and hope that the meeting moves? Miss the meeting and be left out of opportunities? Get help from another family member? But Taylor, for a few moments, feels *unwelcome* at work. While Taylor might have many options for coping with this challenge, the energy that Taylor is spending isn't helpful here, other than to merely return to a normal footing.

Taylor makes it to work for that 8:00 a.m. meeting and finds that the boss's assistant helpfully provided breakfast foods for the attendees. Except Taylor can't eat dairy, and is on a low-carb diet, so none of the foods are safe. Taylor is used to being left out of the meal planning and doesn't know if it was more othering to not have food to eat or to not have even been told there would be food. But it's a distraction to the meeting, so Taylor isn't as fully engaged as possible. At least there is coffee in the kitchen.

After the meeting, Taylor has a few minutes to catch up on email. In cube row, the temperature is a bit chilly, but, fortunately, Taylor keeps a spare jacket handy. Wearing it might slow down typing, but it beats chilly fingers any day.

Looking around, there is no one in the area, but the thermostats can't be manually adjusted. It would take another help-desk ticket, and Taylor remembers being told to just live with the temperature after the last ticket resulted in hours of distraction as maintenance fiddled with the thermostats.

Fortunately, it's only a brief pause and back up to the next meeting. Taylor normally makes sure that someone is done speaking before replying, but this meeting is hard. There are a couple of people who jump right in on the last syllable of the prior speaker, and, even when someone asks Taylor a question, Taylor can't seem to get a word in edgewise. And that morning coffee is starting to catch up! But with three minutes to the hour, the meeting facilitator says, "We've got three more minutes, so I wanted to talk about. . . ." Don't these people have bladders?

By the time Taylor makes it to the next meeting, it's eight minutes past the hour. Someone makes a snarky comment about being late, and there isn't even an open chair available. So Taylor has to go get one from the next room and slinks into a corner with the mismatched chair.

Do any of these sound familiar? Maybe you're Taylor. Maybe you're someone who tried to do something helpful, but didn't realize how the Taylors of your organization might be hurt by it. And these are just the moments of micro-exclusions. Almost everyone feels excluded at some point, in ways that might seem minor from the outside, but still cause discomfort to them. Noticing the ways *you* feel discomfort in a group can sometimes help you see how others feel discomfort from things that don't bother you.

When someone needs to see a doctor on short notice, how difficult is it for them? How about if they go pick up their kids from school? What if they've just been on the road for weeks and need a day to recover? Or they've taken parental leave and aren't quite up to a five-day week in the office? What if they're always the remote member of a meeting, and no one ever talks to them during the premeeting?

Oftentimes, we paint inclusion as an issue for underrepresented minorities, and exclusion can certainly be a challenge for women, racial minorities, folks with disabilities, or anyone who deviates from the "norm." In practice, inclusion is an *everyone* issue at some point or another; it's in those moments when *you* feel excluded that you can relate to another person's high costs. So what do you do about it? Find ways to reduce someone's cost to exist. The easy options are *Pareto improvements*—changes that don't add cost to anyone, but reduce someone's pain. But not all improvements will be that simple; some of them will cost you, or other participants, some energy. But it often pays off.

Do you run a meeting? Set an agenda. Tell people you're starting three minutes after the hour and ending three minutes before the hour; sixty minutes is just as arbitrary as fifty-four minutes, but since our calendaring systems default to sixty-minute chunks, recognize that our coworkers are humans and build travel time and bio breaks into the day.

Are you in a meeting? Pay attention to distributed participants. You can do this reactively, by noticing if someone on a video unit seems to be trying to get in a word edgewise.

Take control in the room, and hand over the attention gracefully. Or be proactive; have a chat window with them or routinely ask for input from participants who are distributed from you first.

Are you coordinating food? Check to see if an attendee has dietary restrictions. People don't always expect you to be able to accommodate them fully, but they'll appreciate you making any effort. If you regularly coordinate food, keep a list of dietary restrictions. My team did this; one outcome we found is that some people enjoy baking for the team, and everyone clearly marks food items with allergen information—not everyone is fed every time, but no one worries about being poisoned.

Are you scheduling a meeting? Learn which people can't be in a meeting early in the morning; maybe they're a few time zones behind, or have kids, or have a morning gym routine. Learn which ones can't stay late—they're a few time zones ahead, or have kids, or they don't work into Shabbat on Fridays. Sometimes, there isn't a good solution. You'll have to pick someone to pay the energy cost. Don't pretend you aren't. Acknowledge their cost. Keep track that you "owe" them, and maybe once in a while schedule around their constraints before scheduling around others'.

One goal of a leader is to maximize the benefit your team gets out of the cost they pay.

> **Inclusion is reducing the energy cost someone has to pay just to exist in a space.**

21

Four days of great work now are rarely more important than four months of good work down the road.

ALMOST EVERY ORGANIZATION TALKS A GOOD GAME WHEN IT COMES to looking after the wellness of their employees. Talk is cheap. Often, wellness is a smattering of programs—often with good intent, sometimes even effective—that nonetheless don't convey to your team members that wellness *really* matters. Organizations might implement program after program trying to patch perceived gaps, but then struggle to understand why those don't move the needle on perception.

The gap is rarely in programs. It's almost always in leadership. A good leader can make a ramshackle set of programs into a supportive net. A bad leader can make a great set of programs look like a Potemkin village hiding a horrible organization. Organizations can hand tools to leaders, but it is up to leaders to implement them well.

As a leader, it's important to truly believe that *wellness trumps productivity*. The benefits you will gain from future work are constrained by your team's future wellness, and extra benefits you can gain *now* are generally at the expense of that future wellness. And while you may often talk about wellness as something important, in the heat of a minor crisis, your leadership actions will often deprioritize wellness in favor of rapid results.

Because the reality is that *you are behind*. There is always more good work to do than people to do it. You know it, and your people know it. When you point at a priority that needs more attention, the very clear message is that your people should work harder. And longer. And that they need to sacrifice their investment in wellness to achieve the organization's goals. Even if you tell them to drop other work, they don't believe you. Why should they? Odds are, the last time they dropped work, you later asked them why that project wasn't further along. And they don't want to disappoint you (or have you angry at them), so they'll figure out how to get it done.

And when you promote the person who risks their wellness the most, you send a clear signal about your priorities.

So what do you do? First, you have to actively model some wellness behaviors, especially if your personal situation doesn't force you to. Your team members with families *have* to set boundaries, so if you're single and relatively healthy, you can actively model doing the same. What are your boundaries between your personal life and your work life? Do you refuse to have meetings after three on Friday? Perhaps you don't schedule meetings from noon to one o'clock, so you can have lunch and go for a walk. Do your people know that you do this? If not, make it more visible. Schedule a medical appointment in the middle of the day, and *tell people you're leaving*. What they see is that it is normal for someone in the organization to establish firm boundaries around their own well-being. That gives them a tool to use for themselves, and use your own practice to show that this is normal organizational behavior.

Next, you have to actively deprioritize work. Figure out the least value-added work your organization does—ask your team, and they'll be happy to tell you—and tell them to stop working on it. If you can't stop entirely, set boundaries for the minimum viable work to keep it limping along, and then *communicate those to your stakeholders*. Let everyone know that this work will not be done, because other, more important, work has taken its place. Say this in front of your team. Put it in writing. Check in regularly, and make sure that work didn't start happening again. "Hey, folks, just making sure that we haven't had anyone pushing to get project X restarted without my hearing about it. That one is still on the back burner."

Finally, you have to actively keep an eye on how much time your people are taking away from work. And make them take *more*. Your people almost never take enough time for themselves, so you have to help them do it. Three-day weekend coming up? Kick everyone out at noon the day before. Someone has a sick kid at home? Make it clear that they can stay home too, and you've got their back. Someone looking a little tired or under the weather? Definitely send them away from work (maybe we'll never be in the office together again, but one person coming into work sick costs you far more lost productivity than the two days you'd lose to bed rest as they get well).

And you have to repeat these three steps *over* and *over* and *over* again, until it starts to stick that you really do care about wellness. And you still probably won't be believed.

Because career advancement is often accelerated for people who work long hours. Even if management thinks they're rewarding only achievement, more hours *generally* correlates with greater achievement. Especially if those extra hours are spent on highly visible work, such as fixing incidents or developing new technologies. That's a challenge you'll also need to address.

But first, keep your people as healthy as you can, physically, mentally, and emotionally, even if current work suffers a small amount.

> **Four days of great work now are rarely more important than four months of good work down the road.**

22

Inclusion is the sum of countless everyday micro-inclusions.

YOU WALK IN TO WORK ON MONDAY AND STOP BY THE CUBE OF A fellow sports fan. You spend a few minutes chatting about the weekend's game—the joys, the heartbreaks—and then continue on into your office, closing the door to spend the next hour reading the email that came in over the weekend.

Sounds plausible . . . and it's also the opening scene in a Human Resources training video covering what *not* to do. That video and training will focus on all of the people in earshot who felt the inequity of being *excluded* by the conversation. Maybe you didn't greet them all, or your greetings felt more perfunctory; whatever your action was, those people now feel excluded. If you press for guidance, the facilitator of the HR training will suggest that you shouldn't have that conversation, that anything that makes someone feel excluded in that way isn't worth doing.

There is almost no action—I'm pretty sure there isn't one at all, but I'm open to the possibility—that makes everyone in a community feel more included. At best, you'll have actions that don't directly affect them, but, nonetheless, someone *may* take offense and feel excluded. That's unfortunate. Even more unfortunate is a reflexive response to not take those actions or to try to water them down to give less offense. Reduced this way carelessly, you not only sacrifice some of the inclusion benefits, but risk creating even more offense.

Consider wintertime holiday greetings. There is a positive trend to acknowledge the existence of more than just Christmas, but just replacing the words "Merry Christmas" with "Happy Holidays" won't achieve your goals. Imagine sending out a greeting video on December 24, with green and gold decor, and nonreligious Christmas instrumental music, complete with a decorated tree, that opens and closes with the words, "Happy Holidays from . . ." That video is *clearly a Christmas video*; as a Jew, I don't feel included by it. But oddly, I feel more excluded by the "Happy Holidays" narrative, *because my holiday isn't even referenced.*

The problem isn't that you were including one group (Christians) too much, so you needed to water it down. The problem is that you didn't create more inclusion opportunities. Send out a Christmas video? Great! What are you doing on Hanukkah and Diwali? Did you do something to celebrate those days, and others, as well? You combat the feeling of exclusion not by excluding everyone, but by including more people.

The same principle applies in the workplace. Sharing a conversation about football creates an inclusion moment with some of your colleagues. You don't have to stop having those moments; what you need is to *create* more moments with your other colleagues. Find out what common activities you might chat about with your colleagues—reading, knitting, parenting, obscure movies—so you can *also* engage with them to create inclusion.

It's okay that not everyone will feel included in every conversation. While those conversations will be evidence that they aren't perfectly included, rather than minimize that evidence, you want to create opposing evidence. Make sure everyone gets included in some of the conversations, so they feel that they are included.

It's the body of evidence that will create the feeling of inclusion. Invest in micro-inclusions, in small ways that help connect people in your organization to you and the organization. Not all of those need to come directly from you as a leader, but you should be seen as part of that pervasively inclusive environment.

Investment in micro-inclusions is also how you keep your organization from becoming a demographic monoculture. One contributing factor to people leaving an organization is feeling excluded. Sometimes, the exclusion alone is enough, but, in many cases, an organization will tend to prioritize the careers of the people the leaders know best . . . which are the people already getting included in a number of small ways. And if you're including people with whom *you* share an activity that you enjoy, then those people are more likely to be like you in other ways.

So embrace new activities and connect with everyone in your organization. Invest in making them feel included, so that you can help them grow to their full potential in your organization. But don't try to remove micro-inclusions; invest in making more of them.

> **Inclusion is the sum of countless everyday micro-inclusions.**

23

Navigating the path forward drives engagement.

Do what I say, not what I do.

—MOST PARENTS, AT ONE POINT OR ANOTHER

"THE CEO WOULD LIKE US TO SOLVE THIS PROBLEM." THAT WAS THE opener to a meeting my boss led with their direct reports. As we began bandying around possible solutions to a difficult problem, our boss shot down idea after idea, only returning to a solution that all of us felt was problematic. About a half hour into the conversation, our boss swiftly shifted away from what we all thought was a conversation, demanding, "Why can't you all just get on board with this solution?" The team ended up frustrated, and the solution was ineffective—either because we were *right*, and the solution was poor, or because we were *disengaged*, and didn't invest enough to make the solution work.

Many of us have been in that "brainstorming" session—sometimes as a participant, sometimes as the organizer—where the output was predetermined; the organizer already had a plan and used a brainstorming session to *re-create the plan from "scratch."* A skilled organizer will do this with great subtlety, and the participants never realize that the solution they've come to was predetermined (often because there actually was only one good solution). A poor organizer does this badly, and the participants end up frustrated, especially if they can see a better solution than the one the organizer had already settled on.

I recall an anecdote told by a peer at another company, which had many large production plants. They'd brought in efficiency experts to redesign the plant processes. At one plant, this included bringing in plant staff to get their input; in the words of the executive, "It was all useless; we didn't make any of those changes." Instead, the company implemented the recommendations of their experts across all of their plants. The plant where they had involved staff? It saw the biggest efficiency improvement of all.

(Note: I suspect that the tale has had some rough edges filed off in the various retellings. I doubt there were no good ideas out of the plant staff; it may be that they overlapped with the experts' recommendations, but the tale remains.)

Both of these anecdotes share a common theme. People who are *engaged* in decision-making processes are more invested in the outcomes, and thus will help make them more successful. *Unfortunately*, both of these anecdotes support a Potemkin village of engagement, because the engagement is only one-way. Real engagement works in both directions.

For easy problems, you can pretend to be engaging with the process as a leader; after all, you've already picked the solution, and you can guide the team toward that solution. The challenge, of course, is not revealing that you're doing so. Because as soon as people realize that the only reason they're part of the decision making is to keep them from arguing later, you'll suffer disengagement.

There are different ways to successfully engage your team. If you have an easy problem, then just delegate it. If there really is only one good answer, let them find it on their own. If there are multiple equally good answers, let them pick one. Letting people choose a path forward is the most sure path to engagement. It's really hard, though. You'll be tempted to predict what the outcome will be. Don't! Even if you have to be part of the solution process, approach it with an empty view and just facilitate your team. When you think they are at a proposal, help them by writing it down.

But if you want long-term engagement? Expose hard problems to your team. Take the challenges for which there are no good answers—you know that folks will push back on you whatever you implement—and let them take a stab at solving the problem. It's okay if they fail to solve it—it's a learning experience for them—but watching what they value at each stage will give you insight in picking a more favorable solution. Seeing the complexity of the problem you had to solve will reduce your team's resistance to the imperfect solution. Removing resistance—the sand in the gears of your team's interaction—is one of the goals of engagement.

Each of these approaches also signals to your team that you value their experience and opinions, in both success and failure. And gives them better insight into how you do your job, which might also give them greater empathy for your challenges. But more important, it allows them to see themselves in your decision-making processes, which naturally creates more engagement.

> **Navigating the path forward
> drives engagement.**

24

People need to see versions of themselves to feel welcomed.

LOOK AROUND AT YOUR ORGANIZATION. WHAT'S YOUR APPARENT demographic breakdown, by gender, race, and ethnicity? You might not be accurate—categorizing others is fraught with peril—but, at first glance, does it look representative of the population? *Which population?* That, of course, is a tricky question. It's easy to convince yourself that your team matches the *qualified population that applies for jobs*, but that is too simplistic of an answer. Diversity isn't just on these few visible axes, but it's a place to start.

As a leader, you have two different responsibilities, *which sometimes conflict*. One is to ensure the diversity of your organization. Separate from diversity—the demographics across your population—you also have to address *representation*, the *visible* appearance of underrepresented groups.

The most powerful argument for diversity is simple: If your organization doesn't have a valid reason to *exclude* certain categories of people, then not having people in those categories in your organization *might* mean you are discriminating against them (you might *not* be, but as a leader, the onus is on you to prove it). That discrimination might not be *active*, but, if, for instance, you aren't hiring women, a simple claim of "it's a pipeline problem" isn't credible.

Another important reason for diversity is being able to see in your blind spots. Having people with different life experiences enables a team to see into places it might not otherwise. This can be as simple as designing for a varied population; creating a restroom hand-towel dispenser that doesn't see melanated skin is a critical failure, and it's less likely that you'll have this failure if there are Black people *anywhere* in your design pipeline. It can be as complex as seeing how your technology could be weaponized in an abusive relationship (if your first reaction to that idea is "my tech could never be weaponized that way," congratulations on being the first technology in the history of humanity to have that feature).

Assessing diversity issues can be as easy as asking a few questions. And then chasing down the uncomfortable answers.

Do your job descriptions disinvite some people? Are you using language that signals an environment that might be unwelcoming to some people?

Do your job requirements unnecessarily filter out candidates? Are you requiring educational experience that is less relevant than work experience? If so, that might select against candidates who've come out of less privileged backgrounds. Do you just have a large number of requirements? There's evidence that underrepresented groups are more likely to select out as you increase the number of requirements for a position.

Do you advertise your jobs in places where people are? If you're hiring out of college, are you recruiting from colleges that have more diverse populations? Or even ones that just have a different population mix than you've historically hired?

When you interview candidates, do they see people who represent a diverse range of body types? People often don't want to be the only person "like them" on a team. That isn't just preference; it's also a signal to them that maybe others like them felt unwelcome and already left.

Do your work hours support people who need different types of work arrangements? If you don't need everyone to be in the office from nine to five, consider the talent pool you can dip into by letting people drop their kids off at school in the morning. Or take public transit to get to work.

That's a few quick questions. If each of them points to a situation where you depress participation by one group by even a meager 1 percent—probably undetectable individually in small to medium communities—it will start to accumulate. And if you have a community that is monochrome, or lacks gender diversity, you make it even harder for the first person to break that barrier, and adding to that difficulty is a form of discrimination.

Diversity isn't just in hiring; it also shows up as a consideration in staff development. However, you *must not* promote someone just to check a box. If they weren't the best candidate, or you promoted them too early, you may instead convince others that *people like that aren't qualified.* You really do want to promote the best. But *opportunity* is where representation shows up as an easier lever to pull. When you're developing staff, are you giving *everyone* development opportunities? Too many development programs start by trying to identify "high-potential" staff. If you invest in developing *all* of your staff, then you aren't relying only on the perception of high achievers, which might be biased in any number of ways.

Hinted at when interviewing candidates is the importance of *representation*. People need to *see* versions of themselves, so that they *believe* that they will be welcomed. If you're applying to a company, and the "Company Leaders" page is entirely white men, would you expect a woman or minority to believe that they will be fairly promoted or mentored? If the only women or minorities are in traditional nontechnical roles, what will that signal to technical applicants?

In a sense, representation is a first step on the path to diversity. If an organization were sufficiently diverse, then, odds are, you *would* see a lot of variation even in small groups. But when that variation isn't there, then you likely have to take active steps.

Consider conferences. In the tech world, conferences are rife with "manels," panels that are entirely men, usually white. Having been on a number of panels (some with varied representation, some without), I think I can safely suggest that not all panel participants are the *best* participants; many panels are formed by the facilitator flipping through their contacts list and calling in favors. But any panel that doesn't include women or minorities—or, worse, *conferences* without a single woman or minority speaker—is signaling to the attendees that those people *aren't welcome in the community*. And not for any good reason. A few panels, maybe with "the three founders of unicorn X," might be tolerable without representation. But that should no longer be the norm.

If you have an opportunity such as a conference, put a finger on the scale. *Every* panel should have at least one woman. *At least*. Realistically, half of the speakers would be women, and significant numbers of minorities would be represented. If you're an organizer, then it's on you to solve this problem. As a leader, even if you're not the organizer, you can make sure that you don't contribute to a representation problem. Challenge the organizers to do better.

Representation shows up in little ways, too. Interview panels should show diverse representation. When nominating people from your organization for opportunities, vary who gets the nod. If you notice that women are always volunteered for one sort of opportunity and men a different sort, switch it up.

It's important that your whole population can see that all opportunities are open to them, as long as they can do the job, and that they won't be excluded because of what they look like.

> **People need to see versions of themselves to feel welcomed.**

25

The best available outcomes often involve finding hard compromises between groups you advocate for.

I CUT; YOU CHOOSE. IT ALWAYS FEELS LIKE THE SIMPLEST WAY TO find a compromise when two people are forced to share a piece of cake. Neither side is necessarily happy with the outcome, but they at least know that the other person *also* had to sacrifice something.

The mental model of cake that makes "I cut; you choose" seem simple is that of cake as being a simple item, evenly divisible. For my young children, that was rarely the case. One of them *adored* sugar and loved frosting. The other really liked the cake—especially if it was chocolate—but would scrape the frosting off and leave it on their plate. A cake could be divided into different parts, and each one would be happier. Right?

Rarely. When their agency was removed, and someone else was now making a trade-off for them—perhaps a slanted slicing where one got most of the cake and the other most of the frosting—they became surprisingly unhappy, despite having a split that was clearly better according to their stated, and observed, preferences. And so as a parent, I'd have to give them "even" splits that were *worse* for them, even though I knew I could do better. Often, they would then be happy to exchange the part of the cake they didn't like for the part they liked. But the mistrust they had of even a trusted agent making that decision for them was too high of a barrier.

Being an *ally* often carries a similar struggle, because you need to advocate for someone who may not be present. Compromise is already difficult, but compromising on another's behalf, without their input? It can feel like betrayal, both to you and to them. As a leader, you're implicitly the ally and advocate of everyone else in your organization, yet you need to make trade-offs and compromises, often without their input, on a regular basis. It can feel like an impossible task. Clear communication helps, and one important thing to be clear on is the difference between practical and impossible choices.

When the company was moving into a new nineteen-story headquarters building, practical requirements on plumbing meant that each floor could have two large multi-stall bathrooms—practically, one for men and one for women—as well as one small room, which could be either a single-occupancy restroom or a "wellness" room (the modern term for what started as a "mother's room," for private use of breast pumps or other needs). One of the many discussions was over how to allocate that room on each floor. An initial sketch of a proposal of alternating floors—so each would get nine floors (the first floor being a different configuration)—stood for a long time, partly because no decision maker felt like they could advocate against either wellness rooms *or* single-occupancy restrooms. But no one felt that the choice was fair, and advocates for different groups were arguing to increase the allocation that most benefited their interest group.

The campus of buildings we were coming out of had *exactly* two wellness rooms, across six buildings, and I do not recall any single-occupancy bathrooms. Almost any distribution was an improvement, but, like dividing a slice of cake, the loss of agency helped create an adversarial relationship. Exposing the decision process and letting people help navigate the decision become essential parts of building trust.

Conversations about what was the best trade-off between the different needs of our population, some of which overlapped, helped us reach a decision that was more accepted. Even exploring impractical solutions helped expose people to more of the constraints on the decision. But it was helpful to listen to stakeholders, both in public and in private, to hear their concerns and explain the thought process.

Your job as a leader is to identify the possible trade-offs in your power and try to optimize for the best outcome. Which might not be the outcome that directly benefits the most people, because sometimes you have to optimize for the needs of the few. Along the way, you need to clearly communicate the options you feel are possible and why you push for the solutions you do.

You will rarely satisfy everyone, but if you listen carefully to the feedback, you can learn what choices might be better to argue for in the future. But a leader has to find ways to help the entire organization improve, while making sure that the same small groups don't always feel the burden of compromises.

> **The best available outcomes often involve finding hard compromises between groups you advocate for.**

26

Performance development should be applied to every person on your team.

Heads I win; tails you lose.
—PLAYGROUND TAUNT

IT'S TIME FOR ANNUAL PERFORMANCE REVIEWS, AND, BY COMPANY policy, there is probably a distribution you are supposed to follow. No more than 5 percent of your staff can get the highest rating ("Greatly Exceeds" or some such), 20 percent can receive the next highest rating ("Exceeds Expectations"), 70 percent can "Successfully Meet" expectations, and, therefore, 5 percent must fall short of expectations. This approach comes out of a philosophy that the distribution of value provided by the members of the organization is fixed.

That philosophy is rooted in the notion of a *zero-sum game*, the idea that in a competition, any advancement by one person necessarily must come at the cost of another person. This idea persists across many domains, and it flavors many of our decision-making processes. If a manager has built a team of amazing people—investing and developing all of them into excellent performers in the organization—they should all "win" with high performance ratings. But in a zero-sum world, there is no notion of "win–win"; realistically, the best split you can hope for is "not lose–not lose" as both sides compromise.

But the reality is that the world is not a zero-sum game. While there is scarcity—resources aren't so infinite as to be free—in most aspects of the world we have not yet maximized the value we can gain from those resources, so we are capable of improving the total value *without* taking value away from someone else. Consider staff development; in this moment, people are a resource, as is management focus on them, and we derive value from their work product. Can we improve the total value we get across our team, by increasing the value each team member provides?

The answer seems obvious: of course we can! But the standard performance-review distribution can't conceive of a world in which we might have 10 percent of the team who greatly exceed expectations. And the usual annual salary adjustment also doesn't take that much into consideration, either. But that doesn't mean you, as a leader, are entirely unable to work on the problem; first, though, you have to accept that, likely, there are headwinds against you.

First, make a list of every targeted professional development program you have, whether it is consciously or unconsciously targeted. Performance management is often focused on our lowest achievers (to drive them out or bring them up to a minimum) and on our highest achievers (to prepare them for their next opportunity). Mentorship programs might similarly go to high achievers. Opportunities are delegated to the people we know are available and can seize the moment.

Organizations invest in managing poor performers out, but the investment is not in improving performance; the investment is spent minimizing legal liability in a lawsuit. Organizations invest in "developing" obvious high performers, but rarely as a means of improving their performance (after all, it's already high). Instead, organizations invest in high performers as a retention signal: "We value you and don't want you to leave. A promotion is coming soon."

Rather than focusing our improvement efforts on actually *improving* performance, we spend most of our energy documenting *why* we are terminating poor performers and a little on keeping our high performers from departing. This laissez-faire Darwinian management model causes managers to implicitly assume that most people aren't going to improve much. This is often compounded by organizations that highly value "player-coaches," managers who started as senior individual contributors and still spend much of their time as an individual contributor. They don't have much energy to spend on any performance management beyond the minimum required.

But those are the places where performance management provides the least return to the team. The middle of your team contains a wide range of people. Some are eager to learn more, but don't know how. Some have great skills, but lack effective direction. Others are quietly waiting for opportunities, but may be afraid to speak up. Each of those people needs a small amount of performance management, delivered to them on a regular basis, to help them become the high performers they may be capable of becoming.

That performance management doesn't need to be aggressive, but it should be continuous and free of surprises. Every person should know what the path is to their next two positions and what skills they need to develop; their manager should know what opportunities are appropriate at this point. When opportunities become available, they should be matched against your knowledge of who needs them, rather than just focusing on short-term success. Mentorship and development programs should go to everyone in a given role, not just to a select few.

Helping one person does not take support away from another person. As a leader, your goal is to maximize the support and value everyone on your team receives, because you want them all to improve, not just a select few.

> **Performance development should be applied to every person on your team.**

27

Your job is not to like your team; it is to not dislike them.

"UGH, WHY DID YOU DO THAT? HAVEN'T WE TALKED ABOUT THIS before? That's so frustrating!" I'm sure that many of us have thought—but hopefully not said—words along those lines before. An employee whom we've worked with to improve a behavior that is disruptive, or to demonstrate follow-through, failed, in a way that was visible, and predictable, and utterly incomprehensible to us. As their leader, we take it personally: we told them not to do something, and we likely told one of our peers we'd handled the situation, and now . . . this. They do it again, *just to spite us.*

And at performance-review time, we often want to make clear our displeasure with their performance. All of their achievements get cast in the light of their failure to meet our expectations. We tell ourselves that *this is for their own good,* and maybe we tell them *this is as hard for me as it is for you.* But it's all a little bit of an untruth. The reality is that it feels good to let them feel our disappointment, not because it helps them improve, but because it makes us feel better. It makes us feel better because we don't like them right now, and we want to make them feel the same pain that they caused us.

Why? Because we feel betrayed by them. We thought we had a friendly relationship, and friends don't let their friends down. And when a friend repeatedly fails us, we don't just become apathetic toward them. We become hostile. And in doing that, we fail at leadership.

Your job, as a leader, is to *lead* people into the future. To help them become better versions of themselves. It's already a really hard task. Most of us also want to be liked as people for who we are and to return that feeling, to like other people. But leadership isn't about being liked or about liking other people. Whether someone likes you is relevant to your leadership only if it helps them become better versions of themselves. Maybe *disliking* you is what is necessary for them. I've had many bosses I didn't *like*, but I was generally able to grow. Sometimes directly with their tutelage, even.

But, as a leader, the one sin *you* absolutely cannot commit is to dislike your people. Whoever they are, you must lead them. Despite their faults, and all their failings, and all the ways you see they could improve but they don't. All of the costs that they incur on your behalf; all of the cleanup work you have to do when they fail. They are still *your* people. You are responsible for them. And as soon as they think that you actively dislike them, they can no longer trust you to lead them. Every action you take, no matter how well intentioned, will be colored by that perception of dislike. They'll wonder if you are trying to help them, or just trying to sabotage them a little more, to further justify your dislike of them.

It's okay if they think that you don't like them *as much* as you seem to like someone else; you don't need to fake being their best friend. But it's important that they can trust that you aren't being spiteful to them. And if they don't return whatever positive emotion you have for them? That's perfectly all right; your job isn't winning popularity contests.

Your people might like you. They might dislike you. You might like them. But that's not your job.

> **Your job is not to like your team;
> it is to not dislike them.**

28

Feedback needs to be a window, not a one-way mirror.

I'VE PARTICIPATED IN A LOT OF PEER FEEDBACK SESSIONS, OFTEN scheduled at the last moment. A meeting facilitator connects participants into pairs, and each gives five-minute feedback to one another. It's a fascinating format; I think its goal is about building connections and demonstrating active-listening skills, but there's something else that I've observed. The feedback often becomes shortened to a descriptive form of name-calling: "You're an empire builder" or "You enjoy picking fights."

For people I've worked with very closely, the feedback *can* be fairly insightful. But for people I've had more casual relationships with, their perception usually feels . . . wrong. Sometimes I can twist it around in my head to find a way to make it fit. But sometimes even that doesn't work very well; the description is at complete odds with the facts I have at hand.

In the early stages of my career, I mostly walked out of those conversations a little puzzled, chalked it up to an odd interaction, and moved on. Until the day a colleague gave me feedback that not only didn't resonate, but was *exactly* the feedback I'd considered giving them, until I realized it would be blunt and harsh and I probably shouldn't say it. And now, of course, I couldn't, really, since it would sound like a slightly more adult version of "I'm rubber and you're glue; it bounces off me and sticks to you."

Often when people give feedback, they're not really giving *you* feedback. They're giving *themselves* feedback. They're judging your actions against their own self-image and then talking about their perceptions of your actions as if they had taken those actions; they're engaging in self-improvement near you. If you're like them, then that critique might be helpful, but if you're not, it seems odd.

Casual criticism is directed at you through a one-way mirror. The giver of feedback sees themselves overlaying a shadow of your actions. The more light that is on you, the better they can distinguish you from their own reflection, but mostly they're talking to themselves.

They see their worst impulses, and compare them to the actions that you took, and see if they can judge you by them. They see their own strengths and weaknesses and assess your outputs against them.

As a giver of feedback, you can overcome this with care, but then you need to recognize that feedback is also *heard* through a one-way mirror. If you have a person who misuses a skill you're strong in, it's very hard to tell them to stop. They see you continuing to use that skill, and doing so successfully, and wonder why you're telling them to stop using it; they see your successful use of the skill as a reflection of their own use of it.

One key approach to giving, and receiving, feedback is to *separate the problem from the solution*. All too often, feedback becomes "Stop doing X" or "Start doing Y," which can suffer from the one-way-mirror problem. That's generally hard to engage with. The Evidence-Effect-Change (EEC) feedback method can help overcome some communication barriers, especially because it removes the shorthand of summarizing behaviors to caricatures.

Feedback is broken into three stages. In *Evidence*, we share the specific, objective actions that caused problems. "You seem to enjoy picking arguments" becomes "In several recent meetings, you and another person spent a significant amount of time arguing over details that weren't getting us closer to a decision."

In *Effect*, we consider the impacts of those behaviors. "Several other people in those meetings approached me and asked to not have you invited to future decision-making meetings, because they felt you were wasting their time."

Change is about the receiver of feedback. While the giver of feedback can suggest improvements, solutions often need to come from the problem owner. "Stop arguing so much" is hard advice to take when someone's role is to provide expertise and counsel. Instead of focusing on specific actions, the giver of feedback should focus on outcomes, such as "I need to have those meetings not be taken over by your arguments." Maybe those are good conversations that should happen in another venue. Perhaps the issues can be written down and considered without a verbal sparring match.

But as a leader, your first goal when tackling a problem is to communicate the existence of a problem. Solving the problem has to come second. Recognizing the communications barrier between humans is critical.

> **Feedback needs to be a window,**
> **not a one-way mirror.**

29

Unsolicited advice
won't always apply.

Just do this one simple trick.
—COMMON CLICKBAIT

WHEN WE GIVE ADVICE, IT IS OFTEN *UNSOLICITED*. EVEN WHEN someone has asked us for our input, they haven't often contemplated exactly what we'll say; in fact, they've likely predicted that we'll give them the guidance that they would give themselves. If they're correct, that's validating their own prediction. But when it's new, and a surprise, it can carry some extra dangers, because they may not be ready to hear it, and we may fumble how we give it. We often aim to communicate with simplicity, and that introduces new hazards.

When we simplify our advice, we often lose valuable nuance. "If you do X, Y will happen" often really means, "For some group (which I think is large, I am in, and I believe you are in), doing X will increase their favorable outcomes in the direction of Y by some (small) amount." Communicating that feels unwieldy and ungainly, so we leave it out. Without those caveats, our listeners may hear us implicitly talking about grouping people together and ignoring people that don't fit into those groups.

When grouping individuals, most people instinctively contemplate an *in-group* (the people who are tightly connected to the source of power) and an *out-group* (the people who aren't connected to that source of power). People have a positive reaction when they feel like they are in the in-group and a negative one when placed in the out-group. Being in the out-group makes you feel like someone *other* than the people who are cared for; few people want to be *othered* out of the in-group. The implicit framing of advice with "if you're in my in-group, this will work for you" can yield problematic results when heard by people that advice doesn't apply to. "I think this works for all humans!" might end up being implicitly heard as "If it doesn't work for you, you're not human." It's hard to make someone feel more *othered*—put into an out-group—than by implying they aren't human.

Most advice also only has a 1 percent effect: for some set of people, this advice might improve their expectations of good outcomes. How big is "some people"? It might be just the advocate ("I did this, and it worked for me"), or it might apply to a larger group. But it rarely applies universally, to every possible listener. Understand that "Just do X to get Y" will feel incredibly unwelcoming to people it doesn't easily apply to: that advice might not work at all for them, or a 1 percent improvement in their outcomes might be outweighed by the odds stacked against them.

That gives the first tip in guiding improvement: acknowledge that you might be wrong and your advice might not apply. And that for some people, these topics are so sensitive and carry so much historical stress that you might hurt them more than you planned to help them.

Consider this one: when people ask how I am, I say, "I'm fantastic!" It helps me keep my frame of mind focused on positives, which increases my resilience to stress. I used to say, "Not bad," and I noticed that I was looking for the bad. Now for me, that "one simple trick" sits on top of a lot of mindfulness, and care, and good fortune. I start by recognizing my advantages: I could have been born a nematode! Instead, I'm really fortunate to be a human in the twenty-first century. I *suspect* that for many people, a daily remembrance of good fortune will improve their condition—but I also know that for people with a wide range of circumstances, from chemical depression to trauma to many more, that advice rings hollow. So when I'm evangelizing something that works for me, and maybe others, I recognize that I am almost certainly talking *at someone* with a different experience. They might not appreciate unhelpful and/or unsolicited advice without caveats.

Recognize that the advice you give might not work for the person you're giving it to, and communicate that uncertainty.

> **Unsolicited advice won't always apply.**

30

Find your blind spots by hearing unbelievable things.

A VICE PRESIDENT IN A DISTANT PART OF THE ORGANIZATION, WITH a reputation for success, was abruptly let go from the company. The rumor mill was hard at work, and the consensus among many executives was that he'd been terminated for sexual harassment. One of my leaders approached me about it, and, somewhere in the conversation, I said, "We have a zero-tolerance policy for sexual harassment."

You know that look you give to someone that is really proud of an accomplishment, but still has a long way to go? A slightly condescending smile, a tilt of the head, and the heavy sigh, all of which combine to say, "I hate to break it to you, but you've got a long way to go"? That was the look she gave me. I read it correctly and was shocked. We'd just fired an otherwise productive leader! Wasn't that a great sign of zero tolerance?

The feedback that I was hearing—that the company tolerated sexual harassment—was *unbelievable*, and I didn't believe it.

At first.

But it bothered me. I trusted the person who was telling me I was wrong. And it was pretty clear that she also believed that I wasn't able to listen to that feedback (she was right). She had a clear idea of how the world actually worked, and it was very different from my ideas of the world. She took a risk telling me that I was wrong.

After a while, I started to wonder. What could be true in her world that made her belief seem correct? If it wasn't true for me, was that because she was wrong or because there were things I didn't see or experience? It would have been easy to move on from this odd interaction, to dismiss it as "not relevant" and proceed. After all, the company had gotten the big picture right, so everything must be okay. I suspect that had been the normal response my team member had received from other managers and executives.

I followed up with her, and I asked for stories. I heard anecdotes, ranging everywhere from things that could be trivial misunderstandings to hair-raising incidents. I wanted to argue, to explain, to justify each story, to give it the context that might make these normal. I tried to keep my mouth shut, so that I didn't stop the conversation. What was important at that moment was learning, turning my head to see what had been happening in my blind spot, and *seeing* the experiences that others were having.

The problem with blind spots isn't just that you miss things that happen. The problem is also that when something slips out of your blind spot, you overreact to it. You deal with a surprising issue that came out of nowhere. You react not with care, but with speed. You tell yourself a story that it was a truly rare occurrence and now you've dealt with it. Meanwhile, things keep happening in your blind spot. But you're convinced that, instead, nothing bad is happening.

Every blind spot you have also leads to worse decision making. Without the context of what others are experiencing, you are likely to say or do things that come across as insensitive, at best. You won't follow up on minor problems, stopping them before they become major ones. The hard part about blind spots is that you often don't even realize they exist.

The people who experience problems in your blind spot have a frustrating experience. To them, you are bothered only if problems get to a certain level; below that, you're apparently fine with how the problem affects them. They lose trust in you, because often *they don't believe you're really blind to what's going on.*

But the world will call out your blind spots, if you learn how to listen. To events that *blind*side you. To people who tell you shocking things. And when you learn to detect the existence of a blind spot, you can start to ask the hard questions, about other people's experiences and what you are missing.

And when you know where problems are, you can find opportunities to improve the situation, rather than waiting until a problem becomes massive.

> **Find your blind spots by hearing unbelievable things.**

31

Make the smallest and most defensible argument necessary to spur action.

TWO PEOPLE DISAGREE. IT DOESN'T EVEN MATTER WHAT IT'S ABOUT, but there is some set of facts that provides evidence to the beliefs that each one has. Usually, neither participant is likely to convince the other; and one contributing factor is that the arguments being made are supported as much by inference and faith as by evidence.

This is the core of the majority of human interactions, especially disagreements, whether it's a pair of children arguing over the fairness of life, political opponents laying blame on each other, or business professionals trying to solve a thorny problem. Both participants are probably right to some extent, but they're probably also wrong to some extent. And humans tend to ignore the weakness in their position while focusing on the weakness in their opponent's position.

Doing so causes us to make arguments that aren't actually as strong as we think they are, because they are held together with cobwebs of hope, inference, and skepticism.

And arguments that aren't that robust won't convince your counterpart, but you can spend energy becoming convinced that the other person is the unreasonable one. Especially when your imperfect arguments get countered with lists of logical fallacies—sometimes fallaciously applied themselves to arguments that are merely stretches, not fundamentally flawed. Attacking only part of the argument, the other person convinces themselves that they've debunked your whole argument, but you only see that they didn't engage your argument on the merits. You may feel vindicated in thinking your counterpart is a fool, but that doesn't move the world further forward, which is probably what you want to achieve.

Let's suppose that you're correct, and you can infer, just from a few hints and pieces of evidence, a whole body of knowledge. But you can't really prove it. And if you bring in that vision of a whole world, the people around you are likely to resist, because they can see the ways in which your vision *isn't* supported by the evidence at hand.

Imagine, if you will, you're in a swamp with some colleagues and you're trying to find your way out. You spot some blazes on a nearby tree and, recalling a history you read years ago, assert, "Friends! We're just a few miles away from the fabled castle of Kludge, where we will be wined and dined by a bevy of wise gurus!" It *might* be true. You *might* be right. But you don't have enough evidence at hand to prove your case. And, rather than getting out of the swamp, you'll now argue with each other, wet, cold, and increasingly miserable.

Sound frustrating? Consider how many conversations look like this. But there is a strategy to make progress. Look at the data you have and consider: What is the *smallest* assertion you can make based on the evidence at hand that is still helpful to the current situation? "Look, folks, someone marked these trees, which suggests there might be a path out of here. How about if we follow the mark far enough to see if there is another?" The goal here isn't to prove anything; it's to shift the group from a place of argumentation and spur them into motion. Once you've achieved motion, then you can begin crafting increasingly broad arguments to continue the motion, because not only have you gained credibility by being correct in a small way, but you've also gotten the group invested in the path they are currently on. That investment makes them more receptive to arguments that justify that path.

That approach is about convincing someone directly, and that works in one-on-one situations. But many arguments take place in front of observers, and those observers are *also* the targets of your arguments. The same basic logic holds true: making minimalist arguments often moves more minds than grandiose claims. But the way in which you argue also affects the opinions of those observers.

Most of us have probably, at one point or another, made the mistake of reading the comments on the Internet, and we've stumbled across the person whom we actually agree with, but makes arguments in the worst possible way—making personal attacks against the observers, using unnecessary vitriol, being arrogant about their rightness. And the thought crosses our mind, "Gosh, they're right, but would they just shut up already?"

Don't be a hint of that person; if your argument isn't ironclad, then having the decision makers choose against you simply because they don't like you is a bad way to go. Instead, your minimalist, well-supported argument, especially in a dispute with a confrontational opponent who makes grandiose claims, will sway more observers into supporting your position.

> **Make the smallest and most defensible argument necessary to spur action.**

32

When mistakes happen, don't waste energy blaming people; invest energy in building better systems.

I'VE LOST COUNT OF THE NUMBER OF INCIDENTS IN MY CAREER that were triggered by human action. Maybe, in copy-and-pasting a configuration line, they left out the last character. Perhaps they used auto-complete to address a message and sent mail to the wrong customer. Or, when making a change, they clicked through a ubiquitous warning message.

In almost every case, someone ascribed the root cause to "human error."

If something goes wrong—really, *when* something goes wrong—our first instinct is often to find the responsible individual. After all, *someone* clearly screwed up, and, even at our most charitable, we should make sure they don't repeat the same mistake. At our least charitable, we want to make them suffer the consequences of their error. Seems reasonable to many people, right? (Not you, of course, gentle reader.)

That person feels *shame*, because they caused harm to the group. The pain from shame effectively neutralizes the person from the environment, as it becomes hard to find a voice in that moment of forced vulnerability. If you're even remotely the culprit, and you're in this environment, what do you do? As soon as folks start looking for someone to blame, you have two basic, and complementary, strategies: find someone else to blame, and conceal your own participation. Accidents become exercises in finger-pointing and blame-shifting, and not opportunities for reflection, learning, and improvement.

Blame becomes *power*. At its simplest form, blaming another allows you to control a group of humans for a moment and to take away another's power. We revel in blaming ourselves in our head and rejoice in blaming others outside our head. But that kind of power feeds on itself; it treats power as a zero-sum game, and you'll believe that you can gain power only by taking away another's power.

That's important to recognize, because *things will keep going wrong*. It's the nature of the universe for bad outcomes to happen and the nature of humans to implement imperfect systems. When those two natures combine, it's a recipe for disaster. Groups that spend their energy on blame move from disaster to disaster, sacrificing their teammates to the whims of a fickle deity of disaster.

But there is another approach to blame, which is to move past it. Recognize that in complex systems, the *proximate trigger* to most errors is a human interaction. The *root cause* (not that there is ever only one) is a hazardous system that was not designed to be safe. If you can believe those two sentences—more important, if you can cause your group to believe those two sentences—then it becomes easier to accept failures and move past blame. The human who triggered the error could even be worthy of praise, for finding a way that the system was unsafe. And when there is no consequence to blame? Then everyone *has an incentive* to be "blamed." The developer who didn't have time to put in enough safety checks. The manager who juggled too many projects and didn't give the developer that time. The process manager who hadn't built in enough controls. The compliance team that didn't notice this hazardous condition.

And with those realizations we can start to learn about what we could do more safely, rather than just scapegoating the unlucky sod who walked into the system. Each person becomes like the blind philosophers studying an elephant. By pooling their knowledge, we can gain better understanding of all of the hazards that contributed to a system, rather than only looking at the one that we think was most relevant.

Accepting blame *creates* new power. In that moment when you show vulnerability, you make it harder for others to pile on and blame you further. You create a de-escalation moment, especially in a healthy ecosystem, because once someone accepts blame, it becomes socially unacceptable to continue to blame them (whereas someone who is deflecting will invite more criticism).

The group dynamics are also positive. Rather than taking away someone else's source of power, you make space for a collective group to stop wasting energy on blame-shifting and start investing energy in building a better future. Groups that accept that bad things happen, and work to minimize them in the future, build better futures.

> **When mistakes happen, don't waste energy blaming people; invest energy in building better systems.**

33

Delegated work won't happen the way you would do it— but it will get done.

ONE OF THE HARDEST MANAGEMENT SKILLS—BUT ARGUABLY THE most important one—is delegation. Why is delegation so hard? Because, most of the time, when you delegate something, it won't be done as well as you would do it yourself. And it won't be done the way you would do it, either. It can feel dangerous to your pride to let a task be done less well than possible.

There are some exceptions to those rules, of course. The US Army invests an awful lot in training its soldiers to be able to make similar decisions in the absence of greater command, specifically so that delegation yields predictable results. That's an outlier case; if you're an Army officer, feel free to skip to the next chapter so we civilians can chat. Sometimes you do have staff who have more expertise and more context than you do, and you'll get better outcomes by leaving them to accomplish a task. Congratulations, you're officially a pure manager now!

But in a lot of situations, the leader is often the technical expert with situational context, especially in fields where the promotion into management comes with longevity as an individual contributor. Delegating work to someone less competent than you are is not an easy task; it requires care, patience, and planning. Even if you have one wonderfully competent subordinate, always delegating to them doesn't allow others to develop their skills. That's also a place where pride can get in the way.

So how do you do it?

First, recognize that the person you are delegating to is, hopefully, not incompetent. They are *differently* competent. You need to understand their strengths and weaknesses, so that you can give them tasks that have both a high probability of success *and* a moderate risk of failure. And then you need to understand what actually constitutes success. It might be "produce a predictable output." But it might be "make this problem go away." Either way, you need to be clear with the person you delegate to how you're planning on evaluating success, so they can work to be successful.

The two opposite ends of the leadership delegation spectrum are micromanagement and completely hands-off management; both of those can be just flip sides of a mismatch between how much oversight a person needs and how much you give them. If you are teaching someone who has never done a task before, of course you're going to spend a lot of time herding them through its steps. But that same level of focus on someone experienced at a task becomes a smothering level of micromanagement. Conversely, asking that accomplished person to do something, and then ignoring them until they deliver the results, might be reasonable, but being that hands-off to a novice at the task is just setting them up for failure.

When you understand how much support a person needs, and how strict the requirements are on the output, you can set people up for success. More important, by not doing the work yourself, you are free to work on new projects. By letting people learn new tasks, you help them develop and grow in their career. Showing people that you can delegate will force others on your team to also start delegating. All of these combine to increase the total amount of work that your team can tackle, even if the way the work gets done evolves over time.

> **Delegated work won't happen the way you would do it—but it will get done.**

34

An apology budget allows your team to take risks.

FAILURE IS HARD. WHEN YOU FAIL, YOU CAN FEEL LIKE YOU'VE LET down the people around you—not just those whom you just failed, but all those who might rely on you. Even harder is when the people that you lead fail, because it's *also* your failure. If only you hadn't left that task to them, things would have worked out better!

Wrong. If you hadn't delegated that work, it, or something else, *wouldn't have been done at all*. And if the people around you are afraid to fail? Then they won't learn by trying difficult things. And that's a much worse failure to your organization than the risk that the delegation fails.

How do you know how much failure risk is the right amount? One approach is to consider having an *apology budget*. An apology budget is just a way to think about acceptable failure amounts; it's the budget for how often you're willing to apologize to someone for a delegation failure. That apology might be to yourself if you're going to have to clean up the mess, or it might be to a colleague who will redo the work, or it might go up the management chain if the work is visible enough. By explicitly considering the cost of failure, you're now able to use it as an investment. You're investing some risk in your apology budget by giving someone the opportunity to learn. Many people learn best through failures and risk of failures; without that hazard, delegating work to someone may not help develop them. How do you know how much of an apology budget you should have? Qualitatively, you can ask yourself, before each delegation, "What's the worst apology I'm likely to have to give when this goes badly?" If the answer worries you, then perhaps add a little more oversight to reduce the risk.

Here's the real trick of an apology budget: it precommits you to *delivering an apology*. Imagine that someone, to whom you delegated work, erred. Not only might they offer up an apology, but as their leader, you might offer two apologies of your own, meeting the standards of a sincere apology.

To your team member: "Look, I'm really sorry that this went south [regret]. I misjudged how much harm we could cause and how much help you might need and didn't give you the right scaffolding to make sure this went well [reiteration]. It was my job to make sure that you were well supported [responsibility]. I should have done better [repentance]. I'd like to understand both how I can better help in the future and make sure I highlight some of your successes in front of the other manager soon [repair]. Can you forgive me [request]?"

To your counterparty: "I and my team failed you on this, and I'm sorry about that [regret]. I overdelegated and didn't provide enough oversight to make sure it went well [reiteration], and that's my fault [responsibility]. I should not have assumed it would work without better oversight [repentance]. I'll make sure that future projects have better oversight, and we can lean in to help clean up the mess we created [repair]. Can we move forward [request]?"

Those apologies feel hard and emotionally expensive. At first glance, they cost us reputation, because they make us look weak. But that cost is really to our own pride, but pride is not only transitory; pride is an *effect* of good work that we do, not the cause of it. Humility is in recognizing that to get better, we have to ignore that moment of pride and pay the short-term cost, in exchange for getting better and having more capabilities.

Maybe you'll simplify the formal apologies according to the situation, but apologies let your partner organization know that you're committed to better relationships and better work in the future and that you stand behind your team. They also make your partner be invested in the development of your team, because you're showing that you're invested in it.

And most important, it lets your team members know that it's safe to be imperfect while working for you and that you'll help them develop in their career.

> **An apology budget allows your team to take risks.**

35

In general, be vague.

"TELL ME, LIEUTENANT, HOW DO YOU PUT UP A FLAGPOLE?" IT'S A classic teaching line, sometimes given to military cadets. It's an open-ended question, which often causes the target to try to decipher the complexities of putting up a flagpole. In that respect, it bears a lot of similarity to many of the standard interview questions popular in the tech community, like "How many piano tuners are there in New York City?" It seems like the questioner is looking to understand your mental process of approaching a problem.

The challenge with off-the-wall questions as a teaching or interview tool is that the teacher is often not really looking for innovative thinking. Instead, they're often looking to see if you answer the question by using the specific thought process that they have in mind. And often, people start to remember the "tricks" for solving this sort of problem, and a question that is ostensibly about innovative thinking instead becomes one about a very specific dogmatic way of approaching a problem. For individual contributors, that *might* be a good approach for that specific problem.

But not for leaders. There is usually only one correct answer to most problems. "I tell a sergeant to put up the flagpole, and then I go do something else."

There's a key to truly effective delegation with a high-performing team, and that's to provide extremely broad directives, with only specific success criteria (maybe you need the flagpole up before the change-of-command ceremony next week!), and then be vague about everything else. If you've built a good team, the team members will leverage their knowledge to solve the problems, often in a better way than you'd conceive of. The more you constrain the solution space for them, by providing unnecessary specificity, the fewer credible options they have for meeting your goals. It's even possible that by being overly specific, you take what was a solvable problem and make it impossible.

When you give people unsolvable tasks, they begin to lose confidence in your ability to lead them. You've demonstrated at least one of several errors. Maybe you don't know what they're good at. Perhaps you don't understand the work you assign them. Certainly, you don't trust them. Maybe you've demonstrated all of these errors, but now your team becomes unresponsive to your needs.

And that's a problem. Teach people to use their initiative. Celebrate when they come up with solutions you hadn't foreseen. If they come back and tell you it's impossible, ask them for their input. What constraints make this impossible? How could you adjust the needs, or give them extra support, to satisfy the goals you most desire?

The further you get from being an implementation specialist, the more your ideas on solutions will develop flaws that you can't see. The more you specify exactly a solution, the less that your team will be willing to point those flaws out. Being vague on details gives people a way to delicately point out flaws in your idea, while still executing on a solution that meets your real goal.

Because ultimately you need to not care about how the job got done, merely that it was done as well as you needed it to be done.

> **In general, be vague.**

36

It's easier to prompt a reaction than an initial action.

MANY PEOPLE STRUGGLE WITH PROCRASTINATION, ESPECIALLY when a task hasn't been started yet. It seems so monumental, sometimes, and the work is unscoped. The upsides and downsides are easily magnified, and while you can contemplate the work, actually starting the work is challenging.

Imagine writing an email to the Board of Directors, or drafting a project plan for some critical work, or even planning a menu for an event. For many people, starting is the hardest thing; plus, the anxiety is real, and debilitating, and should not be underestimated. If you don't suffer from this sort of anxiety, good for you!

When I sat down to write this book, it had already been on my mind for years. A lot of friends and colleagues had told me I should write it; apparently, they enjoyed my commentary on life enough that they thought I should share it with more people (if they were wrong, it's still my fault for writing it, so don't blame them). But even knowing that there was desire, and having spoken publicly about leadership and decision making, sitting down to write this was hard.

Until I realized that I'd already started writing a draft, in the form of blog posts and tweets. I took some of those and put them into one place. I sketched an outline. And I started editing and filling in the gaps. That made the work a lot easier, along with using the Terry Pratchett rule, who famously said when he wrote a novel, "For more than three years I wrote more than 400 words every day. I mean, every calendar day." I aimed for a smaller target of one hundred words a day, so that overachieving was a huge bonus on those days. And this book you hold is no Terry Pratchett novel (if you got this far and still thought it was, sorry to disillusion you).

The more powerful tool was in starting with editing, rather than working from whole cloth. Take one of those initial tasks we dreaded so much: that email, project plan, or menu. What if someone handed you a badly written one and told you, "I need to send this out tomorrow. Could you take a look over it?" Assuming that you weren't out to sabotage the person, you'll probably spend more time rewriting and editing their work than you'd have spent writing a first draft. The output will likely be better than what you would have drafted from scratch. Editing produces more and better output than initial sketches do. Sometimes your goal with a sketch isn't to be *good*; it's to get to the editing stage.

And if this works for you, *you can use it on other people*. Instead of asking them for a project plan, suggest one and note that it's just a sketch. "I was wondering if something like this might work, but I'm probably missing some key dependencies." "I'm not sure what dietary preferences everyone has, but what about a menu that was organized something like this?" "We should probably send an email about the new policy launch, and are these the right high points to hit?"

I call this the Red-Ink Rule. It's easier to get someone to pick up a red pen to correct you than a black pen to help you. And you can absolutely take advantage of that. Take the initial action yourself, and then hand it over to someone else and let them tear it apart and produce something better.

> **It's easier to prompt a reaction
> than an initial action.**

37

Celebrating victories builds relationships.

WHEN I HAD A SMALL TEAM, ALL WORKING FROM THE SAME OFFICE, we'd regularly do team bonding activities together. One day, on a trip to the New England Aquarium, one of our team members picked up a stuffed penguin, and asked her manager if she could expense it. Wisely, he didn't answer yes or no, instead passing the buck: "If you can convince Finance, sure."

She wrote him up as "Office Supplies," and George the Penguin came to work, on the justification that he'd improve morale. His first mission was to visit the manager's desk for a week, as a thank-you for approving the expense report. And then every week, she sent George to another colleague, to celebrate some achievement, no matter how small. After a while, she sent George to visit a colleague in another department, because they'd invested a little extra time and energy in doing the cleanup to finish a security project.

Over time, George visited many of our global offices, picking up body doubles to travel with some of our more visible staff, having his own Twitter and LinkedIn accounts, and colleagues would sometimes go the extra mile to try to get a visit from George. A onetime ten-dollar stuffed animal did more to encourage security improvements than we could have expected. George had built relationships with everyone he visited, and those relationships gave extra benefit to our team.

Rewards are transactions, gifts given for achieving some milestone. They have value, but that value doesn't compound over time. The bonus you give an employee one year becomes expected the following year, so the net value starts to decrease. But *recognition*? Recognition builds relationships, and while relationships do need some ongoing investment, there isn't as much of an expectation of specific recurring rewards.

Recognition can be challenging to implement at large scale, because, ultimately, it's about the energy investment in the relationship. Recognition can be big, gaudy programs where recipients get honored at the annual company all-hands meeting, although those awards risk leaving people feeling left out, especially if the selection process is opaque. Recognition can also be small touches.

Cake is an easy structure for recognition. Did someone complete a major milestone on a CEO-visible project? At the next project update meeting, we'd bring cake, and their whole team could come eat it *with the CEO*. The only extra time we spent was in procuring the cakes (which, given the dietary constraints of the people in the meeting, was a larger challenge than might have been expected); the meetings were already regularly scheduled. The added participants spent a little extra time, coming to a meeting where they heard C-level executives talk about the positive business impact of their work.

The goal is to engage your colleagues and make them want to work with you. It doesn't require grand sweeping gestures; a steady investment in celebrating even small victories along the way builds the relationships for lasting engagement. The energy you invest in celebrating other people's victories is a currency they'll recognize and value. Over time, they may begin to ask exactly how much work they need to do to get the recognition and celebration.

> **Celebrating victories builds relationships.**

38

Don't be irreplaceable;
be unclonable.

ONE OF OUR ENGINEERS BECAME ENGAGED TO BE MARRIED. Usually, that's a call to celebrate. Instead, we had a moment of panic, because this engineer was the person we often gave hard problems to, and they had built many systems to solve those problems. On many of those systems, only the engineer knew how they worked. What would we do if those systems failed during their honeymoon?

Every company has stories of the person who left, and that triggered the long-overdue replacement of a system, since no one knew how the old system worked. Those replacements were, unfortunately, often undertaken at great speed, and shortcuts were taken, all because of the loss of that one "irreplaceable" person.

You might have that person already on your team. The person, like my engineer, who you get nervous whenever they take a vacation. That you're hesitant to promote them out of their current role . . . or, if you do, you're going to move that important work with them. They're an important linchpin on your team, and maybe you give them a little extra bonus or ignore when they take long lunches or cut out early on Fridays (although, really, you should do that for your whole team). But you know how important they are to the functioning of your team, and as a leader, you're terrified they might leave.

Maybe you were that irreplaceable person yourself, and that's why you're now a leader. Being irreplaceable is a path to short-term success; the irreplaceable person continues to get a little bit better at their tasks the more they do them. Since they wrote the entire codebase for that weird internal application, they can fix bugs in minutes and add new features in hours. The lack of documentation, testing, or any of the hundreds of little things that make software engineering into a professional discipline becomes a *feature* of getting to have such an efficient person who manages the project.

The irreplaceable person feels job security; it's literally in the description "*irreplaceable*." They may feel satisfaction in being the only one who can do something. And even the downsides, like being called on vacation to fix something, become a point of pride for them.

But, from a team perspective, an irreplaceable person is untenable. It's like having a giant rock in the middle of your field. It's definitely noticeable, but everything else moves around it. The person standing on the rock has a giant advantage. But for everyone else, it's just in their way.

As a leader, you want *unclonable* people. Each team member should bring a diverse set of skills and perspectives to your team, and *no two people are even remotely alike*. When you find a point of irreplaceability—that one set of knowledge that only one person has—your job as a leader is to fix the problem. Assign someone to follow the person and learn from them. When something goes wrong, *don't* let the irreplaceable person fix it. Make them explain to someone else how to solve the problem, without ever doing the work themselves. Give them an extra vacation, *before* their wedding. Give them time to prepare documentation on how to solve things if anything breaks . . . but you'll only call them on their bonus prevacation. Let them have a real vacation, and, if anything else breaks, ensure that everyone else explicitly knows *not* to call them and learn to live with the problem until they return. Maybe your team will learn how to solve the problem; maybe they'll be extra-incentivized to take more work off your irreplaceable person. You'll help people develop more skills, and you'll free up your formerly irreplaceable person—who may have gotten there by solving hard problems that no one else would tackle—to solve new challenges and further develop their skills.

And when they do inevitably leave your team, it won't hurt your team as much.

> **Don't be irreplaceable; be unclonable.**

39

Create safety to let people warn you of danger.

I'VE BEEN TEACHING MY KIDS TO DRIVE. AS AN INSTRUCTOR, IT'S critically important that I can alert the driver to something that I think they haven't seen. If I can do it calmly, and simply, then everything is good: the driver can quickly react to the changing situation, and everything goes smoothly. If I yell at them, though, bad things will happen. Maybe they'll slam on the brakes or panic in some other way. They'll probably yell back at me, and the tension in the car rises. When I see a new hazard, I have to consider whether it's worth the damage to the uneasy truce in the car to mention it. If I don't mention it, though, it's possible that even worse outcomes will occur.

Projects are a lot like driving a car. There is usually only one driver, although a lot of nearby folks *think* that they are the driver, and they're often doing the equivalent of yelling at the driver to avoid nearby potholes. And when the driver of the project starts ignoring all of those backseat drivers, they get a little more peace . . . until they crash and the project fails.

When projects fail, teams try to analyze what went wrong. In some industries, this is a postmortem, or maybe an after-action review, or even a root-cause analysis. Buried somewhere in the data collected, you'll often find that someone had predicted the failure. Not always in so many words, but they suggested the risk was real. They wrote a footnote about some safety work that should be done. Maybe they sent an email to a colleague. Asked about why they didn't say anything further, they might even be able to name the meeting where they did bring up the topic, only to be shut down.

Once a project has momentum, bringing up risks is a dangerous proposition. Enough senior leaders are invested in the success of the project that they are quick to dismiss risks that are novel to them, often in a way that suggests that whoever brought up the risk is . . . less than competent. They've heard a lot of Chicken Little stories, after all, and the sky never really falls. When a junior team member suggests that something important was missed, and it should stop the project, it's usually a brief conversation. And in that quick exchange, no one remembers the new risk, except the person who brought it up and sees themselves not listened to.

When no one is in the frame of mind to listen for new risks, bringing them up is often a wasted effort at best and a career-limiting one at worst. The very novel risks, however, are the ones we most need to listen to. The person most likely to discover those risks is usually a junior team member—the very person who keeps learning to stop bringing up issues.

The challenge at the heart of these missed conversations is that risk conversations are too often binary. "Should we stop the entire project because of this risk?" is often the first argument heard as pushback when someone brings up an issue. That's a weighty question. Rather than starting a nuanced discussion about how to continue moving forward while adapting to the risk, organizations force a false choice: either the risk has to be so dangerous that it justifies halting the project, or it has to be so minor that it can be completely ignored. Communicating any risk into that framework is fraught with career hazard.

Solving this communication challenge requires creating psychological safety for those junior team members and a change of listening styles by decision makers. Neither of these will come naturally.

The premortem is a helpful tool to solve both issues at once and practice hearing risks in a nonconfrontational setting.

Bringing together your team, ask one question: "Assume that, in a year, we look back on this launch—which, hypothetically, is about to fail—to do a postmortem. What was the cause of the failure?" Now, each team member is empowered—required, even—to share the thing that most worries them. Rather than trying to weigh whether it's important enough to fight to derail a project, each participant can focus instead on the details of the risk. Maybe they are wrong on some key fact and will learn at the moment. Or maybe they aren't, and they uncover a risk that no one had been paying attention to.

I like beginning with the most junior participant in the room and working up from there. No one is constrained by the ideas of their boss, and their topics can be boring or outlandish. The goal is to spur conversation and to hear the voices usually most unheard; let them speak first. When listening, the goal is not to refute the argument, but to incorporate the learning from it into your own worldview. Challenging your own assumptions as a leader is critical; you need to be more invested in learning how the junior team members are right than you are in proving them wrong.

As you practice premortems, you can start to be less formal about the practice. If you can have nonconfrontational conversations about risk in a formal setting, you can probably also start to have them less formally. If you can convince your team that it is safe to talk to you, and each other, about the risks they can see, you begin to see problems early and be prepared for many of the worst problems out there. But as long as they don't feel comfortable telling you about risks they see, the more often you'll end up in a dangerous situation.

> **Create safety to let people warn you of danger.**

Notes for Part II:
Team Leadership

YOU'VE REACHED THE END OF THE SECOND SECTION, AND, BEFORE you move forward in the book, consider making yourself a project plan for how, and when, you're going to implement these lessons. It might help to ask yourself a few questions about each chapter. If you need a chapter list as a reference, the Appendix has the chapter titles with brief summaries, and the Contents simply has the chapter titles.

- Can you apply this skill unilaterally, or do you need buy-in from someone else? Who is that someone?

- How big would the change be when you apply this lesson? Can you break a big change down into smaller steps, or do you just want to leap in feet first? If it's really small, you can just do it.

- Can you try this practice on its own, or do you want to bundle it with something else? Is there a compelling event on the horizon, or on the calendar, that will be a great opportunity to practice this new skill?

- Do you have people on your team who have been asking you to make a change similar to this lesson? Can you co-opt them as allies in helping you practice?

PART III

ORGANIZATIONAL LEADERSHIP

MOST DISCUSSIONS OF LEADERSHIP START WITH ORGANIZATIONAL leadership, but there's a reason this is the third section of the book. Everything you'll find in the next chapters requires you to change the steady state of an organization, *even when you aren't watching it.* This relics heavily on your ability to lead the people you directly interact with, as well as have people further away willing to be led by you, even indirectly. The strengths you've built in personal and team leadership will be the foundation for your organizational leadership.

The changes you will need to make to implement the following lessons will probably take more time. You're working through other people, and it isn't as easy as waving a magic wand, saying a pithy slogan, and watching the magic happen. Organizational leadership has a compounding effect: every lesson you apply makes future lessons easier to apply.

40

You need vision to know
if you're on a right path.

A LOT OF ORGANIZATIONS STRUGGLE WITH ARTICULATING THEIR vision and mission statements, and I suspect that's heavily influenced by not spending time understanding the purpose—dare I say, the *mission*—of creating mission and vision statements. One of the struggles organizational leaders often face is understanding the difference between the two. A mission is what you exist to *do*, while a vision is who you exist to *be*. A mission focuses on accomplishments: what you will do in the world and how the world will be different. A vision focuses on character: how you made those changes in the world and how you will be different. Many competing organizations might have similar mission statements, but their visions can be radically different.

Of all of the organizations I've ever been in, my favorite mission statement has to be the US Air Force's: Fly, Fight, and Win (as a cadet, we'd jokingly refer to it as "Kill people and blow things up"). It's a clean, concise formulation that covers the mission very cleanly: Why do we exist? What are we going to do? What challenges do we take on? Mission is very outward facing; in a corporate setting, you can think of mission as a magnet for budget. The things a company does are the reasons that investors give them money, executives fund teams, and customers pay for solutions.

Vision, on the other hand, is a little more inward facing. It's an aspirational declaration of the choices we want to make on the path to becoming an organization that can fulfill our mission. A well-crafted vision statement is a recruiting tool, a banner that will draw people to join us. When you're drafting a vision statement, start from the sentence fragment, "We exist to be . . ." What comes next? My team at Akamai had a clear vision:

> *InfoSec exists to be a helpful and sustainable guide to a safer destiny—for Akamai, our customers, and the Internet community.*

Notice that a mission is implicitly referenced ("to a safer destiny"), but the vision statement is about who we'll be (helpful, sustainable guides), and who we keep in mind (our employer, our customers, and the world). An important part of crafting the vision statement is to ensure that it is clear and inviting to the most junior newcomers to your organization, rather than simply resonating with an external focus group.

A strong vision helps your managers develop your staff's skills and guides your engagements across your business and customers. A weak vision, on the other hand, will distract your employees. A vision that emphasizes superlatives ("to be the best at . . .") may be muddy because it doesn't describe who you'll become, so your staff members don't see themselves in it. A backward-looking vision, which describes who you are *today*, could be fragile because it's written to capture beliefs that your current long-term staff have about the organization—but it will become a jumble of poorly framed buzzwords. Or a vision that focuses on mission and execution ("to be the most innovative, cost-effective . . .") could be poisonous, because it guides your managers to make poor choices in leading their teams, because its words can be counterproductive to the good organizational culture you aim to build.

The best visions are ones that enable an organization to build a shared identity as part of a team that aims to become something different, and greater, than they'd ever expect. Vision drives identity, and creates a framework for your organizational values, in alignment with your mission. But vision isn't secondary to mission, even if it doesn't directly drive your budget. While mission tells you where to go, vision helps you decide how you're going to get there and who you'll become along the way.

> **You need vision to know if you're on a right path.**

41

Values are the trail markers that keep you on the right path, even when the wrong path looks more attractive.

VALUES ARE THE FRAMEWORK THAT FILL IN AN ORGANIZATION'S vision. At some point, almost every organization realizes it needs to define its values (usually right after it defines its vision). Often, this is reduced to defining some universal human values, like "Be Kind" or "Don't Cheat." In fairness, there are many organizations that might need those reminders. Take Google's original unofficial motto, "Don't Be Evil."

I'm certain that folks in the room thought it was brilliantly clever. Google was going to do good things and wanted just a nudge of reminder. "Don't Be Evil" is a strong value. Your explicit values are written to codify the warning signs for the path you're actually on. By telling its staff to *not* be evil, the signal was that the business drivers would be implicitly pressuring them to, in fact, be evil.

Most organizations don't need to tell their staff that one of their core values is, say, not murdering random people. There are a few that do need to—perhaps you're an actual military or police unit, and "Don't kill random people" should be a value—but that's not relevant for most organizations. An organization's values should be the markers that help keep you on your chosen path and are regularly relevant to decision-making processes.

Values can be, and often should be, aspirational, rather than mission directed. An error that many companies make is to convert their mission into values. *Customer-oriented. Innovative. Cost-conscious.* Those aren't values; those are mission statements. As values, they don't engage your team, because they are already being told to do those things every single day. *Aspirational* values tend to sit in tension with your day-to-day work, and we need to be reminded to pay attention to them.

One way to understand the values you *need* is to ask what you're *bad* at, especially when that's a problem you'd like to correct. Does the pace of work make employees take less time off than they should and neglect their own mental and physical health? Perhaps you need to emphasize the value of *Employee Wellness*, so that both the individuals and their managers are constantly reminded to prioritize well-being. Perhaps your team is located primarily in one location or time zone, and staff in distant locations are excluded as a matter of course. A value of *Global Engagement* can serve as a reminder to consider how to include those staff. You might worry about pressure to make short-term decisions, especially ones that look good to your organization, and thus value *Stewardship*, as a reminder to consider the longer timelines and to prioritize works that might pay off only in the future.

Values can also be a defense against losing one of your strengths. Perhaps your organization is historically exceptionally good at documentation and internal communication. A value of *Institutional Memory* might serve as a catalyst to continue to prioritize work in that space. Or perhaps you are known for showing empathy to people in tough situations, so you might encode a value of *Kindness*. You might be careful about doing work that can create meaningful differences and passing on work that has little value. This might lead to valuing *Effective Change*, as a reminder to everyone to keep their eye on real outcomes.

Those values might not sound catchy. They are effective; those six values were the values I used for leading Akamai's global information security team. We reviewed them every quarter at a team all-hands, so that everyone heard the same words used to describe them. We used them as language when engaging in projects, to make sure we were operating as we had envisioned.

Your organizational values are your defense against the short-term pressures to act in ways that you would, in retrospect, find distasteful. So choose them well.

> **Values are the trail markers that keep you on the right path, even when the wrong path looks more attractive.**

42

You have to feed a culture
to see it flourish.

EVERYONE WANTS TO HAVE AN ORGANIZATION WITH A GREAT culture, one that everyone really enjoys working in and where everyone can thrive. If you put together a handful of great people, you can often stumble into a great culture, but then . . . something goes wrong.

It starts small.

A perk like free soda gets abused, as someone takes a six-pack home every night. Colleagues start to clash when their expectations over workload don't match. Pranks that used to be done in good humor now have a vicious twist to them. Slightly off-color jokes begin to have a biting edge to them. Executives run their meetings over the scheduled time, making others late.

Looking at those examples in print, they seem like tiny, trivial matters. How can such small things destroy a great culture? Much like a spoonful of excrement ruins a barrel of wine, destroying shared trust in a community starts with little problems. One person's minor misbehavior can't be corrected directly if you don't have an intentional culture. Either they are tolerated, which results in damage to everyone around them, or they are corrected with broad and general policies, which damages everyone across the organization.

When an organization is small, and tight-knit, a seemingly good culture can grow organically, without much planning. It grows because everyone in the group knows everyone else and values the history that they all have together. People don't think of taking advantage of the organization, because they see themselves *as* the organization.

As an organization grows, changes happen. New people come into the organization, and they don't know everyone in the organization. That creates a distancing of themselves from the organization, and minor annoyances—things that old-timers accepted with grace from their peers—become burrs that won't go away. Newer people also don't have a shared history with the organization, so they aren't able to disregard those burrs as just a small price to pay to stay with a team they love . . . because they *don't* love the organization.

Take pranking.

In some technical organizations (especially security ones), there has been a history of taking advantage of a colleague who leaves an unlocked computer unattended. Among a small team, perhaps a joking message sent from a colleague to their whole organization offering free coffee gets a wry shrug and a reminder to lock their screen.

Someone new to an organization experiences being the target of that prank differently. They've been publicly shamed. They don't have a reputation yet, and so they start off on a bad foot. They weren't around to see everyone else who had that email sent from an unattended computer; for them, they are the first person to be attacked this way.

Now they don't trust their colleagues. They don't lock their computer to protect themselves against malicious outsiders; they lock their computers to protect themselves against their colleagues. Perhaps they'll start looking for ways to get revenge, to call out their coworkers for *their* errors. But your culture is now swiftly and rapidly heading downhill.

Leaders need to recognize that growing a good culture takes deliberate engagement. You need to determine what norms need to evolve or go away entirely. You need to make that happen intentionally and show everyone on your team—the old-timers whose ways need to change and the newer team members who learn by example—the vision for where the organization is headed.

You have to define what parts of your culture you want to keep and encourage those parts. You also need to recognize that there will be parts of your culture you want to eliminate and actively discourage those pieces. Otherwise, the culture that grew like a wildflower will become a weed as your organization grows.

> **You have to feed a culture to see it flourish.**

43

Keep your hand on the wheel
to stay in your lane.

ONE DAY, AN ACCOUNT MANAGER CALLED ME TO ASK FOR HELP IN managing one of his customers. There had been a minor outage recently, and the customer was upset with the incident report they'd received. I was perplexed at this outcome. I'd written many an incident report for customers myself, and the whole point of an incident report was to take upset customers and make them *no longer* upset. I asked the account manager to send me the report so I could understand what had happened to them.

What I got surprised me. There is a template that all incident reports start from, to make sure that there is common formatting. But in all the places where I'd expect to see interesting explanations about how the system worked, and what went wrong, and what we did to fix it, and what we'd do better next time? All of those sections were empty. Not blank, just full of sentences and words that said . . . nothing.

An incident report is a carefully crafted apology note between two organizations. It's often a bit of fiction, because rarely do you know everything that went wrong in the first twenty-four hours and your commitments to fix things haven't had enough deep thought about them to know if they'll actually work, actually be safe, and, most important, be cheap enough to squeeze into the road map. But almost all of that content was just *gone*. If I changed the date and subject line, this could have been used for any incident. It was about the exact opposite of a good incident report.

I went looking for the incident manager who had written the report, because I was curious (okay, I was actually apoplectic, but I could feign curiosity). How could they send this report out?

They didn't. They showed me the report they wrote, and while it had some rough edges that needed softening, it was a fine incident report. But it wasn't the one the customer saw. The incident manager had written the report, and submitted it for cleanup and review, and then walked away from the incident and back to their day job. And then the report went to a lawyer, whose job was to make sure that anything that actually suggested we were at fault was removed and that we didn't make any actionable promises. It went to a product marketer, who made sure that we didn't disparage any of our products or imply they weren't perfect. It went to a product manager, who took out anything that sounded like a commitment that wasn't on the road map. It went to a sales executive, who made sure that we didn't jeopardize existing customer relationships. All told, it passed through about a half-dozen hands. Each person had one job: to remove content that they saw as problematic.

And when the report came out the other end, they had succeeded. All of the problematic content was gone, definitively, because *all of the content* was gone.

Bureaucracies grow as organizations delegate a limited veto power to small independent groups. That veto power often grows out of a bad incident, and the organization decides, "We'll never let *that* happen again," and hands responsibility for preventing specific bad outcomes to separate teams. Those groups don't have any responsibility to approve, and so their existence is, effectively, to thwart the organization. As a bureaucratic organization gets large enough, the aggregation of delegated-veto teams begins to act at such complete cross-purposes to the mission of the organization that it seems more likely that a villain actually runs the organization, rather than the reality: entire organizations are incentivized to hurt the organization, accidentally.

No one in the review chain for that incident report thought they were hurting the company—but each one had been given only a mandate to remove content. The only way *they* were exposed to risk was if they allowed something to get past them that they shouldn't. And that's what many bureaucracies end up becoming: an accumulation of small groups, each often formed around some bad event in the past, trying to steer the organization only away from that event. But the net effect of all of those small groups is to steer the organization away from any good outcomes.

To prevent this, you need to keep someone in the driver's seat, guiding the organization through the bureaucratic process. In the case of the incident report, the best ones were written by an incident manager who then collaborated with each of those reviewers, so that while words were edited to be safer, the content could remain beneficial. None of those bureaucratic functions *wants* to subvert you, and will often be very helpful if you listen to them, even while you remain in the driver's seat.

> **Keep your hand on
> the wheel to stay in your lane.**

44

Expect what you inspect.

IN 1993, AFTER OUR FAMILY'S INN WENT OUT OF BUSINESS, I WAS fortunate to pick up a gig bartending just up the street at The Equinox Resort, which was then owned by Guinness (I'm sure there is a long story in why they owned exactly two resort properties in the world). One day, the food and beverage manager let us all know about a new program, to support the rollout of the "Classic Six" (single-malt whiskeys from Guinness's subbrand, United Distillers): whichever bartender sold the most in the next month would receive a prize. I don't remember what that prize was, because the program had an added incentive: if you sold at least ninety shots, you'd win either a bottle of Royal Lochnagar Reserve or dinner for two in the resort's Colonnade restaurant.

I spent a month hustling. Anyone who ordered a scotch was upsold. Already ordered one? I made sure you ordered another. The regular who dropped by in the afternoon? I made sure he had one of the preferred whiskeys before he got to the bar. I was a few short as the end of the month approached, so I bought the last needed orders out of my own tips.

Yes, I won that competition. Somewhere in a file folder, thirty years later, I still have that gift certificate for dinner, since I never redeemed it (The Equinox having changed hands multiple times, it is well past its validity). I was really excited about it, until a few days later, when the same manager who had rolled out the program called me in to tell me that they were very disappointed in me. That I'd been *too* aggressive at selling.

In hindsight, I suspect that the goal of the program had not been to sell the Classic Six at a very high rate. Perhaps the manager had expected that, whenever someone asked for a scotch, the bartender would suggest, "Have you heard about these lovely single-malt scotch whiskeys? Would you like to try one today?" and, if the patron declined, the bartender would move on, but the brand-awareness moment would have happened. Maybe the patron would try one of the whiskeys and discover a new one to pick up at the liquor store.

It's really hard to measure the output we want, so we often settle for measuring the output that was easy. The output I suspect Guinness wanted was a positive brand moment for their whiskey line. The output that they could measure was sales at that bar. By measuring sales, they got sales. The ninety new shots of whiskey I sold in a month, compared against worldwide sales, were negligible. But how many patrons did I turn off from even trying these? Or, having tried them, developed an aversion from the high-pressure sales tactics? Guinness may have received a negative brand moment from the very program intended to produce a positive brand moment.

As a leader, we often have to rely on secondary measurements of the outcomes we really desire, but we often fail to understand how we're incentivizing the behavior of our staff and whether that incentive drives in the exact opposite direction of our goals. There's a classic *Dilbert* cartoon to this effect—if a software company financially incentivizes fixing bugs, a developer can make a tidy bonus for themselves by *introducing* easy-to-fix bugs.

Diversity programs often suffer from the measurement effect. Imagine telling your leaders that you're measuring the representation of specific groups. What you probably wanted was a program that actively recruited great candidates from outside your normal hiring pipeline, and identified the ways your organization might have previously driven away those candidates, so you can fix those problems. What you'll probably get is managers who functionally implement quotas or engage in discriminatory hiring or retention practices (perhaps your HR department, during a layoff, actively challenges terminations only from specific groups; it's a clear signal to your managers to discriminate against other groups). Instead of fixing one large problem, you've created two large problems.

Whatever you measure, you're going to get *more* of—either the direct item measured or the activity around that measurement. As a leader, you have to anticipate how that will go wrong and watch for places where you should stop or alter a measurement program because it isn't incentivizing what you actually need to improve on.

> **Expect what you inspect.**

45

If you don't pay attention, you'll miss the gorilla in the room.

THERE IS A WELL-KNOWN EXPERIMENT DETAILING THE SELECTIVE attention test (which I'm about to ruin for you if you've never seen it). Christopher Chabris and Daniel Simons have a video, with two sets of humans, one wearing white T-shirts and the other wearing black T-shirts. They have basketballs, and the viewer is instructed to count how many times the group wearing white shirts passes the basketball to one another, as both groups mill about seemingly aimlessly. About halfway through, someone dressed in a gorilla suit walks through, pauses, beats their chest, and walks off. A surprising number of people, when viewing the video for the first time, completely miss this large and unexpected interloper.

Viewers are told to watch for only one thing, and so their attention isn't available to notice other issues. Similarly, in an organizational setting, if your leaders are repeatedly told about one priority, but only occasionally told about a second, then the second priority will get very little attention. And soon, it's not a priority at all.

"Unlimited" time off has become one of the more recent management trends, for reasons both good and bad. *Vacation time*, as an accrued entitlement, creates a liability on a company's books. As an asset for the employee, and a liability for the employer, vacation time creates a lot of problems. If an employee leaves early for a medical appointment, the employer is incentivized to make sure that time is accounted for (reducing a liability on the books), while the employee is motivated to do the exact opposite (protect their vacation time), and neither one is incentivized to meet in the middle.

Enter Unlimited Time Off. Of course, it's not *really* unlimited, but the idea is brilliant. Rather than employees having to carefully micromanage a bank of vacation time, and worry about keeping enough in case they get sick, you instead allow them to take as much time off as they need, *as long as they get their job done* (let's come back to that in a moment). Now if an employee needs to take a day off to deal with an automobile repair, they aren't worried that they can't take a week off to go to a tropical destination next month. If they take an extra hour at lunch for a medical appointment, no one is counting the minutes. Employees might actually take breaks and recharge, rather than hoarding those scarce vacation hours. In theory, it's a beautiful idea.

In practice, it's a nightmare. Because employees are no longer *entitled* to their vacation times, it's easier for a manager to justify *not* approving time away, because the work isn't done. Deadlines have moved up. Shifting requirements have stacked up work. Besides, that employee just took three half-days to take care of their kids! Even though the organizational leader just stood up at a team all-hands meeting to talk about the importance of time away, managers also hear all of the important things they're directly responsible for (after all, it will affect their bonus, so it's quite personal), and they're going to make management choices that are exactly the opposite of what you might want them to do.

Values are one approach to tackling this mismatch. If managers are making choices that directly go against your stated values, you can *hope* that your staff will have the courage to point this out. But that hope is nurtured only if people have seen you respond to violations of your values. And it's a passive leadership approach, waiting for something to go wrong, rather than keeping an eye out to help it go right.

You need to keep steering your organization forward, in the direction you're aiming for. You'll need to ask how a policy might be misimplemented, and what you'd expect to see if it was, and then actively go looking for it. Unlimited time off? How many days a year do you expect the average employee to actually take off? How many per quarter? Start monitoring, on an ongoing basis. Maybe you expect that most employees will take some time throughout the year, but with large chunks in the summer and winter. But you're looking not for maximums, but for minimums. Are there teams that aren't taking enough time off and aren't planning ahead to take off time that you'd expect?

If you don't keep your eye on the processes of your organization, whether it's time away, measuring the recruiting pipeline, or tracking promotion and progression opportunities, you might be inadvertently incentivizing poor choices to your leaders. Choices that you'll be uncomfortable with when they come to light later. If you want something to be an important rule, you can't just tell people once; you have to make sure you are inspecting the process to keep that rule at parity with everything else you ask of them. Otherwise, they'll be paying attention to the minutiae and not notice when something else goes awry. And, by inspecting, you'll teach the leaders in your organization that you're really serious about the values of your organization, and you'll teach them how to help your organization become better.

> **If you don't pay attention,**
> **you'll miss the gorilla in the room.**

46

From a distance, any sufficiently complex system is indistinguishable from a simple system.

THERE'S AN OLD SAW ABOUT A RETIRED CUSTODIAN. WHEN A BOILER stopped working, his former employers called him up and asked him to come back in and show them how to fix it. He arrived with a piece of chalk, put a small X on the side of the boiler, and told them to hit it with a hammer. They did, and the boiler started working again.

He sent them a bill for $30,000. Surprised, they asked for an itemization, and he responded:

Chalk: $5

Knowing where to mark the X: $29,995

It's a fun joke about the value of deep systems expertise, but it highlights a separate issue about the complexity of a system. From a distance, we often think of a heating system as a very simple system: it takes fuel, creates heat, and transports the heat to the places we need it. At the level of a campfire, that's not an inaccurate model. As we add little bits of complexity to our campfire, we can hold the complexity, as we think about airflow, stones to capture and radiate the heat, and means to redirect smoke away. But at some point, the system becomes so complicated that, unless we have deep expertise in the system, our minds just see a simple system again. And, to fix problems, we think we just need to bang it on the side and it'll work again, . . . but it takes deep expertise to understand *why* banging it on the side might work.

The challenge as a leader—especially if your expertise is similar to the expertise of the people around you—is that when you see a broken system, the experts who know it better than you do *have already tried to fix it*. And if your expertise follows the same paths as their expertise, everything you're going to suggest is something that they've already discovered won't work.

There's a communication challenge involved here as well. A system is currently broken, and experts have already spent significant time diagnosing the problem and trying to fix it. They bring it to you and give a quick summary of the problem, leaving out all of the dead-end paths they've already tried. Seeing a simple problem, you helpfully suggest, "Why don't you just . . . ?"

"Just."

That one word creates more harm to your ability to lead your organization than it might seem. You've suggested that the people who work for you are foolish, that they can't see the obvious in front of them, and that you're so much more clever than they are that with only a moment of thought, you can solve problems that baffle them.

And with only one word.

It isn't unreasonable to check that they have tried the obvious, but you need to be explicit that you are just verifying, not assuming that they didn't ("I assume you've already tried X, Y, and Z?"). It's fine to ask *why* something didn't work, because you want to learn more. And when they tell you something preposterous, you need to take a moment to believe them. A response like "That can't possibly be true" to an explanation about a challenge tells your organization that you cannot be trusted with uncomfortable truths.

As an organizational leader, you need to trust that your organization is full of competent people and that they mostly don't need you. If you don't have that trust, then your staff will stop trusting that you will add value when they do get stuck. They'll seek ways to stop engaging with you, because the simple solutions you push on them cost them more energy than it takes to work around you.

Start with questions that demonstrate that you understand the limits of your knowledge. "Maybe I'm missing something, but why wouldn't X help?" Take their answers as authoritative. Even if you don't quite believe them, follow up later. "How can I help?" is a powerful question. What your team needs from you is probably something outside their purview: getting help from another team, getting permission to do something outside the norms, or preparing for an escalation. What they don't need is to have you oversimplify their problem and waste everyone's time.

> **From a distance, any sufficiently complex system is indistinguishable from a simple system.**

47

Whether you jump out of an airplane or get pushed out, you still need a parachute.

BEING IN THE RIGHT PLACE, AT THE RIGHT TIME, WITH THE RIGHT solution: ultimately, that's the objective that any leader should have for their organization. Doing so reactively— waiting for something to go wrong to prepare to fix it—is almost impossible. By the time you've identified the needs, it's too late to address them. Success requires being prepared *before* you know you need to be prepared. Much like finding yourself on the outside of an airplane. Having a parachute makes you successful; whether you planned to jump or were thrown out of the plane is irrelevant.

I used to oversee Akamai's incident-management process, so I've had a lot of experience in the fundamentals of incident response, which starts, continues, and ends with "Move fast." Movement in a good direction was a requirement, but a good move *now* was generally preferable to a better move *tomorrow*. Often, those good moves were identified by discussing scenarios in advance.

For many organizations, disaster planning often revolves around predictable or expected events. Yet the most agile individuals and organizations often look well prepared because they're willing to contemplate the inconceivable in advance. In contemplating it, not only can they face adversity with grace, but they can begin to assemble the components of a rapid-response plan. Plans don't necessarily need to be comprehensive in advance—that much work for every contingency would be overwhelming—but should contain the set of initial steps to take in a crisis, a decision-making process for future steps, and enough components of future steps to enable the swift assembly of a just-in-time, comprehensive plan.

Including outlandish possibilities can often provide a fresh look at some essential steps, as well as providing an opportunity for a bit of levity. Many years ago, when I was in charge of our business-continuity planning, we assembled a rather vague and mundane set of emergency plans for our operations center. These plans were contingent on whether our building was functional (power and Internet), whether our building was accessible, and whether our people were able to work.

With three distinct inputs, we had eight different scenarios to plan for. Which worked well, until one day a very particular auditor complained that we hadn't actually defined real scenarios and demanded that we describe an actual emergency for each scenario. It came time to define a scenario where our building was functional and our people were able to work, but the building was inaccessible for an extended period of time. We contemplated putting in the mundane "snowstorm" scenario, but anyone who has ever had to stay home during a nor'easter knows that most of your employees are busy removing snow from their properties and productivity plummets anyway.

We settled on a slow-moving zombie uprising as our scenario. We posited that our employees would be confined to their homes, but somewhat able to work, and that our building would still be functional. Then we did genuinely explore our plans for how we would operate *in a zombie apocalypse*. Every subsequent auditor was impressed with our foresight, and it was an inside joke for many years.

Yet the elements of our zombie-uprising plan were serious and sound and wound up informing our decision making in other events. After the Boston Marathon bombing, residents were asked to stay home, the FBI established their mobile command post outside our headquarters, and our employees were prepared for how to work remotely. At the start of the global COVID-19 pandemic, our staff was again prepared to move quickly—even if no one expected it to last as long as it did. Neither of those events was predicted, but we were, nonetheless, prepared to tackle those surprise incidents as if we'd prepared for them for years.

Because, in a sense, we had. Having found ourselves on the outside of an airplane, I was glad we'd already packed a parachute.

> **Whether you jump out of an airplane
> or get pushed out, you still need a parachute.**

48

There is no perfect plan— there is only the best plan so far.

ON A REGULAR BASIS, MY WIFE TURNS TO ME, AND SAYS, "SHOULD I do X or should I do Y?" Sometimes, she's asking me what meal she should have for lunch. Maybe it's about what outfit to wear tonight. Perhaps it's about making plans for our vacations. I used to think really hard and deeply about giving advice to her, and I found it really stressful when she seemingly disregarded the very advice she'd asked for, sometimes in the blink of an eye.

One day, I realized that I wasn't actually being asked for advice. I was being asked to be a reflective sounding board: she needed someone else to propose an answer so she could examine her own gut reaction to the idea. If she liked it, she went with it. If she didn't like it, she went the other way. But she needed another person to propose the idea, because otherwise she couldn't step far enough away from the proposal to consider it; if *she* proposed it, now she was invested in its success, even if she didn't like the idea.

So now, when I'm asked, I first consider whether I care about the outcome. If I don't care, I mentally flip a coin and give an answer. Maybe I lead with the alphabetically first answer. Or I take the most outlandish answer. It doesn't matter; what matters is that I quickly give her an answer so *she* can make a decision.

Because what she's really doing is taking a step back from analysis paralysis. The reality is that there are many good choices in the world; in the grand scheme of things, either choice is comparably good. Attempting to identify a perfect choice often results in indecisiveness and more pain for everyone around. In a moment like that, there is far greater value in just making a decision than in making a *better* decision.

Decisiveness is the art of actually reaching a decision. You need to recognize that the time cost of improving a decision can be a problem for you and the people around you, that the longer it takes to make a decision, the worse off you'll be, even if you get to a "better" choice. One approach, above, is to trust your instinctive reaction between two choices, by picking one, and then seeing if you want to switch decisions. If so, go for it!

But what if you have an unbounded number of choices? You're brainstorming new ideas, and the universe of choices makes it hard to simply compare them all. Another approach is to imagine, if you will, that your choices are M&Ms. And the "best" choice is the *hardest* M&M, which isn't easy to spot at a glance; you have to test the M&Ms, and the easiest way to do it is to compare two M&Ms: squeeze them together. Whichever one breaks clearly wasn't harder, so just eat it now (yum!), and the other is a better candidate for best M&M.

One way to find the hardest M&M—er, best idea—is to organize a tournament, like a sports league. Pair up all the M&Ms, and test each pair. Then repeat until you only have one M&M left. It's effective, but if you absolutely can't finish, you have no way to compare the remaining M&Ms. All you know is they aren't the weakest M&Ms, but if you randomly pick one, it doesn't have any argument for its being better than any other M&M that remains. If you'd only done one round of tests, then each M&M is better than exactly one other M&M. After two rounds, they're each better than three, then seven, then fifteen. But you're randomly picking from what's left; all of the tests that promoted M&Ms you didn't pick are wasted effort.

A different approach is to pick one M&M. Any one, it doesn't matter. This M&M is the best M&M *so far*. Now, if you have any time remaining, pull out another M&M and compare it against the current best. Whichever one wins is now *the best so far*! And you can repeat this, until you need to make a choice.

The best part about this model is that every test matters; you're always comparing your current selection. At any point, you can stop and have confidence that the choice you're making is a good one. And those comparisons are targeted; you aren't comparing hypothetical plans. You're comparing your actual plan against a single alternate at a time.

When you're making a decision, you can refer to your current best plan as "your M&M." You're signaling to yourself, and others, that you're still willing to change your mind and reminding yourself that a better M&M might come along. But if it doesn't, you've got a decision ready to go.

> **There is no perfect plan—**
> **there is only the best plan so far.**

49

Act faster than your adversaries and slower than your allies.

IF YOU'VE EVER WATCHED A MOVIE LIKE *TOP GUN*, **PERHAPS YOU'VE** seen a military aviator tell a story. They raise both hands. One is their plane, and the other is the enemy's. As they tell the story, their hands gyrate to emulate the maneuvers of each pilot, as each tries to gain advantage over the other. Key to this storytelling is the reaction time of each participant: how much more quickly one can get from observation to action is going to determine whether a pilot wins or loses.

Business leaders, for better or worse, often follow military-themed mental models, and acting quickly to stay inside your competition's decision loop is a common theme. "Acting quickly" isn't really the best description of optimizing Colonel Boyd's paradigm of decision making; it's ensuring that by the time your adversary gets around to acting, you've already changed things, possibly through a fast action, so that their action is ineffective. Organizations tend to celebrate rapid decision making as conditions change, and, in many cases, this can be a good thing. If the market changes, you'd like to act before your competitors do. If you sell a security system, you'll be more successful if attackers can't adapt more quickly than you do.

Unfortunately, habits like this—move quickly and surprise your adversary—become a routine that is used even when interacting with internal peers. And those collaborators certainly shouldn't be considered your adversary. But if conditions change slightly and you act quickly and surprise them, especially if you had an aligned interest or "deal" you're now ignoring, they'll certainly be made to feel like an adversary.

The goal of a good organizational leader is to make sure that your partners can predict the actions that you and your team are going to take. That puts *them* inside *your* decision loop, and now they can feel like they have the upper hand. That creates trust for them, in that you won't surprise them (if anything, they get to feel empowered to surprise you). At the same time, of course, moving too slowly might be dangerous to your own standing in the organization, so balance will be key. You are better off improving their reaction speed than just slowing yours down.

Begin by removing the secrecy from your planning process. As soon as you can see that the situation is changing, make sure your partners are aware. If you *think* that the situation might change soon, you can casually talk to your partners about that potential change and idly make contingency plans with them. This starts their decision-making loop much sooner, which will significantly reduce the discrepancy between your decision making and theirs.

Remember not to make decisions *for* your partners. Let them make decisions, even if you already know that they'll be able to respond in only one way. If you walk in and share a decision with them, even if well supported by a chain of ten well-reasoned arguments, they'll feel like you're leaving them behind. But if you bring in nine of those ten well-reasoned arguments, and then *together* you explore the tenth argument, and then *they* propose the decision, you've let them reach action ahead of you. Sometimes, you'll end up with the same decision you'd already come to. But many times, with their input, the decision might be better, even if in only small ways. But, even more important, your partner is now bought in on the decision, and they're less likely to engage in passive resistance.

Sometimes you'll have to weigh the consequences of just abiding by a previous decision and not reacting optimally to a changing circumstance. Your partners might not see or believe in the changes. Or they might be constrained by other needs. Or the cost to them to change course is just too high right now. Whatever the reason, sometimes it will be better to successfully execute an in-process imperfect plan than to disrupt everyone with a more perfect plan that has no chance of success.

> **Act faster than your adversaries
> and slower than your allies.**

50

Skill balance is essential to managing crises: technical skills to directly change the world, people skills to change the world through others, and process skills to keep the world changed.

PEOPLE OFTEN TALK A LOT ABOUT "SOFT SKILLS" AND "HARD SKILLS." I've always disliked that split, because it sounds not only vague and artificial, but somewhat demeaning. Who would ever want to specialize in being soft, like a pillow? I prefer to think of skills grouped into three categories: "technical," "people," and "process."

Technical skills include what most people think of as "hard skills." It's the skills of doing work and changing the world yourself: writing code, graphic design, systems administration, building a house. These skills tend to be *measurable*, so we call them hard, because we understand how to train them, and often there is a hierarchy of skill competence. And while the computer industry has laid claim to "technical skills," any skill by which you directly change the world is included, from various trades (construction, plumbing, and so on), through support staff (from janitors and housekeepers to receptionists and customer service), to creative work (artists, graphic designers, and writers). Realistically, these are the *simplest* of skills to see in action: they are the set of skills by which we directly translate our will into a change in the world.

People skills are skills that let you work through other people, that enable them to do work for you: management, communication, coaching, cheering. They're harder to measure, partly because there is rarely one "right" way. So they are called "soft," not because they are easy, but because their definition is so truly nebulous, as well as environment dependent. You can't manage all of your people the same way, which is very different from realizing that, generally, you're going to frame walls in the same way wherever you're building a house. But people skills let you change the world by translating your will into *someone else* changing the world, so they are a multiplier on your own capabilities and help increase their abilities as well.

Process skills are those that let you work through an organization: process design, operations research, user experience, and project management. These are even harder to measure, since their effects are often disconnected from their application. So we often don't even name them, possibly catching them gently under the "soft skills" rubric. But process skills are the most powerful, because they let you translate your will into *people that you don't even know* having effects on the world, even when you aren't around.

Most individual contributors and low-level managers often develop depth of excellence in only one of these three areas. Of course, that generally means those people will most value the skills that they specialize in and denigrate skills that they don't have. But as their career grows, the limit on their effectiveness is generally whatever they are *weakest* in. In many organizations, this often results in feeling impostor syndrome quite often. An engineer who makes vice president should spend most of their time on managing people and processes, not doing technical work. The technical work they *do* engage in will often be oversight of other contributors. Whereas a pure manager, as they move to vice president, may struggle with the lack of technical expertise—even in an oversight role—that constrains them.

That form of imbalance also means that the more senior a decision maker is, the more likely that their models of appropriate solutions are going to be oriented to the strength of their own skills, often ignoring their weaknesses. Many organizations promote based on the organizations' strengths: a technical organization is likely to promote based on technical excellence, a people-oriented organization is likely to promote based on people skills, and a process-oriented organization will promote based on process skills.

There is an advantage when organizations have a bias toward a set of skills: most challenges that that set of skills can address will be easily handled. If a technical approach to a problem is reasonable, then a technically oriented organization *will* find a workable solution.

As unsolved problems escalate to more senior levels, however, the more those problems are likely to need solutions that are oriented *away* from the organization's strengths. When the senior decision makers also share those same organizational strengths, they will look to apply solutions that junior staff already tried and failed with. And leaders may be reluctant to hear from more junior staff that they aren't actually as brilliant at solving problems as they think they are.

It's in that moment, when a problem needs to be solved with skills outside an organization's focus, that a leader with a balanced set of skills is most likely to succeed and add value.

Process, people, and technical skills all have different applications. Individuals can specialize and have a great career. But having strength across all of them is where your organization can become powerful, especially in solving problems by having skills outside the norm for your team.

Whatever skill your organization is the weakest in is the skill most in need for events that become crises that senior leaders have to deal with. Learn to value the skills that you don't have, to keep those crises at bay.

> **Skill balance is essential to managing crises: technical skills to directly change the world, people skills to change the world through others, and process skills to keep the world changed.**

51

Embrace the heroism
of boring maintenance.

IMAGINE YOU HEAR A STORY OF A SCHOOL BUS DRIVER WHOSE BUS
went over the side of a cliff. The heroic bus driver managed to skid their bus down a steep incline, through a rocky
ravine, narrowly dodging disaster, returning to a road below,
all while keeping all of their charges safe.

Wow. Sounds improbable, more like an action-movie
sequence than anything we'd see in real life. Told in a group,
everyone will laud the bus driver's excellence, heroism, and
quick thinking. And rightfully so. Just as when Captain Sul-
lenberger landed his plane on the Hudson River, we marvel
at the amazing things that humans can do in times of great
crisis, and we are happy to have such heroes in our midst.

Some organizations move from incident to incident, celebrating at each turn the heroes who narrowly avert disaster.
These organizations embrace *hero culture* as a way to survive

in turbulent times. That celebration becomes an incentive: teams seek to hire heroes or to find heroics that they will be cheered for.

But what about all the school buses whose mechanics noticed a problem and pulled the bus from service until it could be fixed? Or the highway engineers who ensured a guardrail was on all of the dangerous spots? Or the drivers who drove a little more carefully on curves? Aren't they heroes, too? Don't they save as many, if not more, lives?

Indeed, their efforts are also laudable, even if we never name them. They rarely see themselves as heroes, because their effort isn't extraordinary *to them*. They're just doing their job, and the way in which they did their job, with no fanfare, had the same—or better—positive effect as the heroic tale, at far lower cost.

And that's the true downside of hero culture. By focusing all of our celebration on the massive energy output that mitigated great harm as it was happening, we start to minimize an organization's perception of the value of the work that provides greater safety at scale. And that carries with it several costs.

Organizations don't prioritize the boring and mundane work that staves off future incidents. No single piece of work is so amazing as to justify itself, and so those organizations create *more* opportunities for heroics by increasing their own hazards. And incidents are, generally, expensive. They do cause harm, even in the best of cases. Those children on the school bus that went off the road are traumatized by the experience, even if they didn't suffer physical harm. Your customers still lose confidence in you each time you have a (short) outage. And your staff are definitely harmed each time you disrupt their routine to deal with a problem.

If you organize your team around incident support, then you will build a team of people who can't get time flexibility. You're going to exclude the people who can't drop everything on a Friday night or who have outside commitments. Maybe you'll hire them, but it'll be harder to give them opportunities when they have coworkers who are always there for you. That disparity will start to show up in unbalanced demographics.

People who combine incident-paced work with a normal schedule of work also have a hard time recharging, because incidents often take away their normal downtime, leading to further stress in the organization.

As a leader, you need to create space for your team to fix problems long before they might happen. Doing so will not only lead to fewer incidents; it will also create a healthier culture for your organization to thrive in.

> **Embrace the heroism
> of boring maintenance.**

52

If you aren't regularly failing at future bets, you aren't taking enough risk.

ALMOST EVERY SPORTS FAN HAS THAT MOMENT IN THEIR FANDOM when they yell at their team. Not for losing—that happens all too often—but for being ahead in a game and playing not to win, but to not lose. It's a subtle distinction. Whether it's the "prevent defense" (American football) or "four-corners offense" (basketball), armchair coaches often lament that what it does is prevent *winning*. And, to some extent, they are correct.

The game-theory approach of playing not to lose is, when ahead, to trade off the margin of victory to reduce the possibilities that the other team has to win. A 50 percent chance at a resounding win, with a 25 percent chance of a moderate win, turns into a 90 percent chance of *just* barely winning. And, on paper at least, that can make sense, especially when winning and losing are binary. It's frustrating to a fan base, and coaches are sometimes wrong about the probabilities, but, in games, it can make sense—when the final score doesn't matter, isn't it better to win 90 percent of the time, with an embarrassing defeat 10 percent of the time, instead of winning only 75 percent of the time, even if two-thirds of those wins are amazingly dominant?

In business, though, the final score does matter. Success isn't binary. Rarely do you want to trade great victories for mediocre ones, but risk aversion around the risk of failing shows up even more readily. For decades, the mantra in the IT industry was "No one ever got fired for buying IBM." As long as you make a decision *just like everyone else does*, even if you don't succeed wildly, it won't be the end of your current employment.

Unfortunately, this mentality can permeate your organization. People don't get promoted until they're perceived as ready to do the new job. Products are launched on time, but with only minor incremental improvements. Companies make "safe" acquisitions of businesses that have established themselves, paying a higher price than had the acquisition happened a few years prior.

At heart, all of these are the business equivalent of playing not to lose. When you play to win, you accept that sometimes you'll fail, need to apologize for the failure, and move on. But if that isn't culturally safe in an organization, then instead of taking the bigger risks that provide bigger returns, your organization will increasingly take smaller and smaller risks and succeed by smaller and smaller amounts.

Adjusting this mentality requires careful diligence and planning. Counterintuitively, measuring a minimum acceptable failure rate in processes is a way to succeed by creating an incentive to fail *quickly*. All too often, organizations behave as if there are a limited number of bets they can make, and therefore all of them must be curated to victory. In reality, the sooner you recognize that a bet *isn't* going to pay off, you can declare it a failure and place your bet on something else.

A product-launch process could be turned into a funnel: Concept Exploration leads to Market Analysis, followed by Product Design, which drives Engineering, which leads to Launch. There are more phases, but looking at those five phases, there are gates before each one, whose driving purpose should be to *fail unsuccessful ideas*. In many organizations, being the product manager on a failed product is a career-limiting move, so each individual has the goal to *make sure their product gets past the next gate*. That success may come by redefining the product's goals to make it seem successful, even if it's no longer the success it needs to be.

Looking at that product-launch process, each gate, whether it's the decision about which ideas get to enter Concept Exploration or which Designs lead to Engineering, should have an expected failure rate. Ideally, gates early in the process should have high failure rates, while later on gates should have lower ones. Ideas are cheap, so throwing out 90 percent of them isn't that expensive. Throwing out 90 percent of your systems right before Launch, however, means there was a lot of waste; a 5 percent failure rate might be more reasonable. With expectations of failure set, now an organization can measure to make sure failure is happening *at least* as often as expected.

Not all bets need to be big gambles. An organization should mix in safe, incremental bets with high-risk, big-payoff plans. And those might have different expected failure rates. But it's easy to tell if you're making bets. The best sign of bets is that you don't always win.

> **If you aren't regularly failing at future bets, you aren't taking enough risk.**

53

Failure is an opportunity to provide great customer service.

WITH AMAZED DISAPPOINTMENT, I LOOKED DOWN AT A PLATE OF ravioli. I had told the conference organizers that my dietary restrictions were "no dairy, no egg, no pork, no shellfish," and it seemed pretty clear to me that "cheese ravioli" wasn't the right meal for me. The hotel staff insisted that this was the meal that had been ordered for me, but they quickly pulled together a plate of steamed vegetables so I at least had something to eat.

In a moment of pique, I posted a quick photo of the "meal" on Twitter and named the hotel (I was tired, and hungry, and I was still learning how to be a better leader).

A half hour later, there was a tap on my shoulder. A very *apologetic* hotel manager was there and explained that they'd been told I was a vegetarian. They wanted to know what my actual needs were. The chef came out and asked what I would like for each meal (the steak, cooked rare, at dinner the next night made me the envy of the conference). When I returned to my room, there was a plate of fruit (no cheese or dairy chocolates) as well as a split of champagne. When I got home, I received a lovely handwritten note, along with a hat and shirt from the hotel.

The hotel could have taken the attitude that the meal screwup wasn't their fault—and I've been at a lot of conferences where the venue followed that approach—but they chose not to. In a moment of failure, rather than focusing on blame, they focused on fixing the problem in the best way they could. And in that moment, they could succeed in a way that they would be unable to without the error.

Without failures, it's very difficult for an organization to truly excel at customer service. Even great customer service becomes expected, and your customers may notice good service, but, like driving along a paved road, the lack of potholes is rarely commented on. But once a failure happens, attention becomes focused. Your organization might have caused the failure. The customer might have caused the failure. Someone else entirely might have caused the failure. But now that the failure has happened, and the customer is in distress, you have an opportunity.

How you perform in that moment becomes amplified to the customer, *especially* if what you're doing is unusual.

Great customer service after a failure is unusual. Especially when the failure isn't really your own fault. It's always easy to justify why the customer is wrong or try to return to normal operating procedures as quickly as possible. But when you do that, you leave a lingering dissatisfaction with the aggrieved customer. If, instead, you take a few extra moments, as an organization, and not only solve their problem but also give them a great experience, they'll remember the story for life.

And this applies not just to traditional customers, but to everyone: your staff, your colleagues, your acquaintances. An employee is having a dissatisfying experience with the HR department? Interceding on their behalf will stand out. A colleague is having a frustrating time interacting with your organization? Stepping in to mediate the confusion goes a long way. Seizing the opportunity to help people when they're having a difficult moment will always be a powerful positive experience.

> **Failure is an opportunity to provide great customer service.**

54

If you spend all your time fixing current crises, you aren't averting future crises.

THERE'S A CRISIS TREADMILL THAT MOST ORGANIZATIONS TEND TO operate on. First, something goes wrong. Springing into action, teams across the organizations work really hard to fix the problem—or at least make it no longer noticeable. Having just barely recovered, you assess the "root cause": that one thing that seemed to be the most obvious driver of the problem among a dozen other things that contributed. You implement a quick fix to the problem, often by yelling at the person who stood closest to the problem when it happened. Taking a deep organizational breath, you return to normal, hoping that you have a few weeks until . . . nope, something else just went wrong.

This never-ending treadmill isn't building up capacity to manage crises, because the people on the treadmill need a break. They might be gaining skills at crisis management, but when they can't take a break inside the organization, they'll take a break *from* the organization. While that's a bad problem, it hides an even worse concern: incident response rarely improves the overall situation for a company. It certainly recovers from a bad spot, but the hazards that contributed to or created the problem? They rarely get fixed that easily.

Crises come about when many things go wrong. Many of the things that went wrong happened long before you noticed the crisis. Consider tending a garden. A crisis might be something like "a rabbit just had babies inside my lettuce patch" or "there's a creeping weed strangling my rosebush." If you quickly spring into action, you can remove the rabbits or pull the weed. You might lose a day of productivity, and maybe that exact problem won't come back up again. In a little while, perhaps some chipmunks are eating your strawberries, or your roses look a little insipid, and you're back at managing the crises that interrupt your routine gardening.

What you're missing is that those incidents are all related. Your vegetable bed isn't protected from any wildlife and needs a whole host of security systems added. Your rosebush is casually planted, without mulch or the right amount of water to the soil, so weeds keep attacking it. When something goes wrong, often it's helpful to take a step back. The impulse to work really hard for a few moments "just until we get back to normal" is tempting, but often it is effort that is, in the long run, wasted. And habit forming, because it *feels* more successful than it is. If you take a step back, you can consider all of the hazards that contributed to your current dilemma.

No organization is going to fix all of the hazards that expose them to risk. But few organizations are willing to deeply and honestly look at all of them. Every impulse to notice human error can be a prompt to look at the hazard of missing automated systems or quality controls. Every quick, simple story about how the system "just" needs a quick fix is an opportunity to look more deeply and find even minor contributing factors.

Having a list of all the hazards that contributed to one crisis isn't enough justification in most organizations to solve all of those problems; there are too many to solve them all at once. But having that list serves two purposes. First, you'll start to *expect* certain crises, because you'll recognize that when you "fixed" the previous crisis, you left the system in a dangerous state. More important, you'll start to recognize the subtle problems that, while never appearing to be the direct trigger for any crisis, are merely present as a contributor to many crises. And having taken the time and energy to find those ever-present hazards, you can spend time fixing those, rather than doing just enough to get back on track . . . momentarily. And that will be time well spent, protecting your time and energy in the future.

> **If you spend all your time fixing current crises, you aren't averting future crises.**

Notes for Part III:
Organizational Leadership

CONGRATULATIONS ON REACHING THE END OF THE BOOK . . . BUT the start of the rest of your journey. Applying the lessons of the final section can be the most challenging . . . and the most gratifying, when you see changes cascade through the organization. Take a little while to observe your organization, because it will tell you, although not always in words, which lessons you most need.

- When you have that internal "face-palm" moment ("Why did so-and-so do that?"), ask yourself if any of the lessons you've just read apply. How would they? How are you going to introduce the concept to your team?

- When things are going right, which chapters are closest to describing what's happening? Can you strengthen that practice, even by 1 percent, to make it more predictable?

- Which chapter leaped off the page for you? Write down the chapter title on your whiteboard or on a sticky note. How many times a day do you get to observe it? Who can you talk to in your team to celebrate it or to implement it?

- If you're going to recommend *1% Leadership* to any of your colleagues, which chapters will you suggest they read first? Why?

Appendix

You're still here? It's over. Go home. Go.

—FERRIS BUELLER

CONGRATULATIONS ON MAKING IT THIS FAR! IF YOU JUST SKIPPED TO the end of the book to read this, well, congratulations on skipping ahead. Writing this book has been a journey for me, and I hope that reading it has been an easier journey . . . so far. Getting to this point took a half century of leadership lessons from the people around me, and many of these lessons I'm still working on today.

If you're done with the book, I hope you found some wisdom in here that will help you improve your own leadership by 1 percent, and then another 1 percent. . . . Perhaps you'll come back to the book from time to time, revisit some of these lessons, and dig in more deeply. Maybe you'll discover the lessons that I missed here (I'm not so arrogant to claim that there are only fifty-four lessons to be learned, or that I know them all). Maybe one of these lessons resonated so well that you'll amplify it and share it.

Perhaps every week you'll come back to the book and try to improve based on one of the chapters here. You can share those ideas with your team (the chapter titles are intentionally designed to be shareable, like pithy notes on a whiteboard or just a comment on social media). You can even give your teams copies of the book, which both I and my publisher will thank you for. However you choose to improve, and share your improvements, I wish you success in your efforts.

The real secret of leadership is that we're always trying to pass it on. You're not just trying to become a better leader; you're trying to make the people around you become better by your presence. You're trying to make the organization you build be a stronger one when you leave than when you arrived. And, if you can do that, you'll have succeeded as a leader.

If you need a quick reference, and the Contents wasn't enough for you, here is the list of chapters, with a brief explanation of my intent in writing each one.

Part I: Personal Leadership

The first main section in the book is "Personal Leadership"—how you use your will to improve yourself.

1: Personal improvement is a prerequisite to leading professionally. Leadership is more than just telling people what to do: it's showing them how to be and allowing them the space to be better versions of themselves. To do that, a leader needs to demonstrate that personal growth is acceptable.

2: Your attitude is in your control. Recognizing that the way that you interact with the world is largely driven by how you choose to see the world, a leader can improve their own attitude by choice.

3: Your blessings exist only if you remember to count them. It can be simple for a leader to always focus on the problems that confront them. Remembering all the things that go right will provide context for the bad days.

4: Becoming right requires accepting that you might be wrong. All too often, we are convinced of our own correctness and ignore even minor flaws in our arguments. By acknowledging the possibility of being wrong, we not only learn faster, but invite collaboration.

5: Even if you don't succeed, a story about failure can be a reward. People often focus just on the learning aspect of experiences that go awry, but it's the power of storytelling that reinforces that learning.

6: Gift kindness where it isn't expected. When kindness is unexpected and unnecessary, joy is freely given; by surprising someone else with a positive moment, you can improve both your world and theirs.

7: Don't borrow evil where it wasn't intended. All too often, we interact with other humans as if they are adversaries, casting them in the worst possible light, to justify our own less-than-perfect behaviors. Learn to look at our counterparties with a positive assumption.

8: An uncompelled apology unburdens everyone. Too often, forced apologies are used as a form of power currency, rather than as a means of soothing conflicts. Unforced apologies lead to more rapid forgiveness.

9: Regret is an act of forgiveness to your past self. When we can forgive ourselves, we can focus our energy on making better choices in the future.

10: Stop visiting your Museum of Past Grievances. We aren't the only ones who have wronged us in the past, of course, and carrying that hurt can be harmful to us. We need to stop carrying a continuous reminder that makes us spend energy on unhelpful, negative thoughts.

11: The only thing keeping you from having more fun than you are having right now is you. Take moments of joy where we find them, rather than worrying that we aren't acting seriously enough.

12: Make expensive time worth it. Having joy is especially important when we've paid a high cost for the time we have, or, more important, when someone else has paid that cost for us. Misery *doesn't* love company, and the greatest honor you can give to someone else's sacrifice is to make it worthwhile.

13: Your wellness is one of the greatest assets you control. That holds true for physical and emotional wellness. The value you provide to an organization is almost always limited by your wellness—it's a piece of the human capital you draw on—and it's a key investment everyone should maintain.

14: Retain the confidence of the new learner, and temper it with the caution of the old hand. We may have both over-confidence and the feeling of being an impostor, and it's in balancing those two ideas that we both try new things and learn from the imperfections as we try them.

15: To engage in the present, be of two minds about the future. As we try things, sometimes we are faced with near-certain failure, and the path to success seems nearly impossible. Worrying about failure will make success even more unlikely. Only by engaging in the present without that worry can we find the path to success.

16: Practice the future to face adversity with grace. We can prepare ourselves for those moments when our shock might cause us to react in a fashion we might later regret.

17: Helping others is an investment in helping yourself. Even when we need help, focusing on helping others gives us a reprieve that allows us to restore our own energy.

18: Serenity is knowing that the crap you're wading through is crap you chose to deal with. We may have chosen to take a path that has a cost that we might not appreciate, but recognizing that we chose this path can give us the serenity to endure.

Part II: Team Leadership

The second main section in the book is "Team Leadership"—how you use your will to improve those around you.

19: Leadership is helping someone become a better version of themselves. Leadership isn't about getting more out of your team; it's about putting more into them, which generally results in getting more out of them. But you can't put the cart before the horse.

20: Inclusion is reducing the energy cost someone has to pay just to exist in a space. When someone doesn't feel welcome in a space, even for minor reasons, they spend more of their energy focusing on protecting themselves and less on being part of the team. Giving them safety and welcome increases their available energy.

21: Four days of great work now are rarely more important than four months of good work down the road. Most people can spend extra energy to get a little more work done right now, at the cost of getting less work done in the future (or leaving entirely). Show that long-term wellness matters.

22: Inclusion is the sum of countless everyday micro-inclusions. Inclusion comes not from some grand sweeping gestures or from the elimination of micro-exclusion; it comes from continuous and small signals to people that they also belong in a space.

23: Navigating the path forward drives engagement. The more your team has visibility and input into the hard decisions you have to make, the more their empathy will drive their engagement. When people can't see the difficulty of a choice, they will readily criticize the trade-offs without empathy.

24: People need to see versions of themselves to feel welcomed. It's not enough to merely be diverse; to attract and inspire people from different backgrounds to you, they have to see that people like them have been welcomed and supported.

25: The best available outcomes often involve finding hard compromises between groups you advocate for. Not all paths forward involve perfectly positive improvements. Sometimes, you have to make compromises as a leader that you can't make as merely an ally.

26: Performance development should be applied to every person on your team. Rather than treating the performance process as a way to identify and document poor performers, create a process that aims to improve and develop every person on your team.

27: Your job is not to like your team; it is to not dislike them. Many management guides focus on the harms of being friends with people who work for you—but there is much more harm to be had in active dislike of a person who works for you.

28: Feedback needs to be a window, not a one-way mirror. The goal of feedback should be to let someone see how their actions are viewed from outside their own perspective. Too often it is a criticism, comparing them to their reviewer's idealized self-image.

29: Unsolicited advice won't always apply. When you give unsolicited advice as a directive, being wrong harms a relationship, so make it a conversation starter, acknowledging that you might be wrong about it.

30: Find your blind spots by hearing unbelievable things. Sometimes, the most unbelievable statements you hear aren't indicative of delusions on the part of the speaker, but point at an area where you have so little knowledge, or too much comfort, to see problems that you should address.

31: Make the smallest and most defensible argument necessary to spur action. It's easier to do nothing than to do something. That gives people a strong incentive to find flaws in arguments, so make the smallest, tightest argument that achieves what you need, rather than wasting energy defending unnecessary and weak additions to your argument.

32: When mistakes happen, don't waste energy blaming people; invest energy in building better systems. Systems that are unsafe provide a lot of opportunities for humans to trigger bad outcomes; if you waste time and energy blaming humans, it makes it harder to lead the progress to improve the system.

33: Delegated work won't happen the way you would do it—but it will get done. There's a lot of good work to be done, and insisting that it all be done to your specifications is a way to ensure that less happens. Get more done by trusting people to get it done in *a* right way.

34: An apology budget allows your team to take risks. Your team will make mistakes. Ensure they are willing to stretch themselves by demonstrating that you'll have their back and take the fall for their errors.

35: In general, be vague. Be specific only about things that matter.

36: It's easier to prompt a reaction than an initial action. Starting from nothing is often a daunting task; when asking someone else to do new work, you can spur their efforts by giving them a flawed first draft to work from.

37: Celebrating victories builds relationships. Humans want to be valued, and investing small amounts of energy in their successes will tell them that you value them.

38: Don't be irreplaceable; be unclonable. The set of capabilities you bring to your team will never be replicated in another person, but nothing you do should be done only by you; teach those around you to do the things you do, which frees you up to learn to do new things.

39: Create safety to let people warn you of danger. The high cost of speaking up means that teams often accept unnecessary risk. Creating low-cost ways to signal that a risk is present will keep a team healthier.

Part III: Organizational Leadership

The third and final section in the book covers the hardest, but most valuable, part of leadership: "Organizational Leadership"—using your will to improve those *far away from you.*

40: You need vision to know if you're on a right path. Many organizations think of vision as an idealized view of themselves, considered from an external perspective, rather than using vision as an internal view of themselves—still idealized, but based on the desire of the organization to move in a specific style.

41: Values are the trail markers that keep you on the right path, even when the wrong path looks more attractive. The best values are those that create tension in the organization, not because the values are weaponized against junior staff, but because they constrain the whims of the managers in the organization.

42: You have to feed a culture to see it flourish. It can be relatively easy to stumble into a good culture, but to have it last over time requires deliberate, intentional investment.

43: Keep your hand on the wheel to stay in your lane. Bureaucracies will tend to subvert their own implicit goals unless you explicitly counter that tendency. Left unattended, a large organization will easily take the words of its leader not at face value, but at an implied message that is almost exactly the opposite of what was intended. Good leaders need to examine the outputs of an organization to make sure it remains aligned.

44: Expect what you inspect. While it's important to measure your outcomes, a culture that emphasizes its measurables will get more of what it measures—even if what you're measuring isn't exactly the value you want to get.

45: If you don't pay attention, you'll miss the gorilla in the room. If you want something to be an important rule, you can't just tell people once—you have to make sure you are inspecting the process to keep it on track. Otherwise, they'll be paying attention to the minutiae and not notice when something else goes awry.

46: From a distance, any sufficiently complex system is indistinguishable from a simple system. A system that works smoothly will, to an outside observer (like you), seem much simpler—and easy to "fix"—than it really is. Learn to trust your experts who are closer to a problem when they suggest that simple solutions are less appropriate than you believe.

47: Whether you jump out of an airplane or get pushed out, you still need a parachute. Being prepared isn't about anticipating the future; it's about setting your organization up to be nimble and ready for many possible futures, so you can swiftly pivot to adjust to a new reality.

48: There is no perfect plan—there is only the best plan so far. Rather than trying to create a perfect plan, always have the "current best" plan. This counterbalances the tendency of larger organizations to always hunt for a perfect plan.

49: Act faster than your adversaries and slower than your allies. While you want to be more agile than your adversaries, if you are visibly more agile than your allies, you'll surprise them in unpleasant ways. Give them time to catch up to you before you move again.

50: Skill balance is essential to managing crises: technical skills to directly change the world, people skills to change the world through others, and process skills to keep the world changed. Whichever skill your organization is weakest in is the skill that will create the most problems, and thus you'll need it most in a crisis.

51: Embrace the heroism of boring maintenance. You can stave off the need for Herculean efforts by investing in keeping problems from happening in the first place. It's boring, but more valuable.

52: If you aren't regularly failing at future bets, you aren't taking enough risk. It's easy to have a perfect batting average if you're always batting off of a tee. Beating risk is where organizations provide the most value over their competitors, which requires taking risks. If you aren't failing, you might be too risk averse.

53: Failure is an opportunity to provide great customer service. You can provide good service only when someone is already having a good day. It's in the moments when someone is having a bad day—even one you caused—that your organization has an opportunity to provide *great* customer service.

54: If you spend all your time fixing current crises, you aren't averting future crises. Crisis response consumes a lot of energy in an organization, and it not only distracts from making forward progress, but deflects energy from the boring maintenance work that will avert future crises. Prioritizing based only on urgency creates more hazards in the future.

Acknowledgments

WHY DID I WRITE YET ANOTHER SELF-HELP BOOK? A LOT OF PEOPLE around me through the years have said nice things to me about the random advice I've given them. Some of that advice has made it onto Twitter, or occasionally onto my blog. Some of it has shown up in presentations I've given. This started as an effort to see if I could distill down the wisdom I've received from others (which most of this is, even if some of it has been by counterexample) into something that others can share.

But a few helpful people have stood out along the way. My wife, Gisele, who pressure-tested more tidbits than I'd care to admit, many of which were discarded along the way. If this book is like a child, then she's as much its parent as I am, even if I spent more time in labor on *this* one of our offspring. Without her, this book doesn't exist, because the person who wrote it wouldn't exist, and I'd be a very different, even less wise, version of myself.

For Mom and Dad, who probably tried to get even more nuggets of wisdom into me than you'll find in this book, but I was sometimes a little too thickheaded to hear and remember the lessons you tried to give.

For Lila and Isaac, who had to listen to a lot of rough drafts of these nuggets in car rides and over dinner tables and gave me some new ways of looking at these lessons.

For the rest of you, alphabetically:

To Arianna, who, when I shared an anecdote about recognizing how fortunate we are, told me I should be sharing more widely—specifically, with NFL locker rooms. She's not the first person to tell me to share, but that conversation one day was like a seed pearl, irritating me until I sat down to write this book.

To Ashley, whose courage in telling her story, and willingness to let me reshare it, both breaks my heart and makes it more full.

Dan, who saw the potential in this book and jumped in wholeheartedly.

Daniel, who is absolutely not a nematode and whose comment has stuck with me for years. If I needed reminding about how to enjoy life—sometimes in apparently reckless and dangerous ways—you've always been an example.

Jeff, to whom I, and all of my readers, owe Bruce a deep debt of gratitude for introducing us. You have been the crucible that distilled this book into its reality. Some of these gems needed a lot of polishing.

For Joan, who one night called me the most interesting man she'd ever met, only three-quarters tongue-in-cheek, I suppose, which gave me the confidence that others might find these stories and epigrams interesting.

Kathryn, whose incredible patience is matched only by her obstinate belief that there was almost always a better choice, if only you could find the path to unblock it. And whose many long conversations—in which we didn't always agree, but I always found insight—lay the groundwork for parts of this book.

For the countless scholars who've done the real research that I've merely skimmed from, and cherry-picked, to build a model that worked for me. Some I can remember: Rachel, who reminds me in my head that cognitive models might be informed by scientific research, but that "science says that" is a really dangerous formulation even for a professional scientist to say; Gary, who I didn't realize was *that* Gary until we were hanging out in our sukkah one year; Nancy, whose work is on a path that was tangential for long enough to really stick with me; and Bill, whom I still haven't convinced to come work with me . . . yet.

To all of my coworkers across my career, who each contributed in some way to my thinking about these topics: thank you for your patience as I've learned.

To the Friends of George, you know who you are. Each of you wrote some part of this book. I'm merely the scribe performing interpretive keyboarding for the people who weren't in the room when it happened.

To the Friday therapy group, who got to have many of these essays dropped in at (hopefully apropos) times: your responses definitely showed me which essay titles needed rewriting.

And to all of the Peloton instructors, who drop random tidbits of wisdom in their classes, while giving me something to focus on while I improve my health.

To my early-draft readers, for taking a swing at me, and giving me a lot of comments, most of which, I promise, I didn't ignore. But any problems that still remain are my fault. Thank you all: Amy, Barbara, Brian, Fadi, Frank, Jeffs (all three of you), Jennifer, Wim.

To my publishing team, this book is remarkably better for your help. Thank you to my personal A-Team (Amber, Alison, and Annette, plus whoever jumps in after my final edits).

To all of you who have read the book: thank you for the trust you've shown and the energy you're about to invest. Without you, there isn't a reason for the book.

Thank you.

Index

About the Author

I HAVE REFERRED TO MYSELF IN THE THIRD PERSON ALL TOO OFTEN in my professional career, but not today. My career has wandered through construction, hospitality, teaching, military service, website design, software engineering, cybersecurity, investing, and, most recently, marketing (which would startle a younger version of me). I spent more years kicked out of MIT than I spent at MIT. I have managed at a lot of levels, from a shift foreman to a C-level executive, and now divide my professional time between advising security startups, mentoring CEOs, writing op-eds (and, apparently, books), and speaking on topics from leadership to cybersecurity.

You can find most of my other works—podcasts, public talks, op-eds, blogs, fanfic, and a more formal bio—curated on www.csoandy.com. If you enjoyed the book, or have questions, or want to connect with other folks who've enjoyed the book, I'd love to hear from you, either on Twitter

(twitter.com/csoandy) or LinkedIn (https://www.linkedin
.com/in/csoandy/) or Facebook (https://fb.me/1Percent
Leadership). If you'd like to inquire about engaging me for a
book signing, keynote talk, or leadership consulting, you can
connect at sales@duha.co.